Mailed It!

"Ashley and Dayana practice what they preach, delivering a book as clear, concise, and relevant as the emails they teach you to create. They build trust through honest, intimate communication of their own triumphs and mistakes and leave you not only smarter, but more confident to make the most out of your own email communication."

—DAVID DYLAN THOMAS, world-recognized public speaker, content strategist, podcaster, and author of *Design for Cognitive Bias*

"Get this book. Read this book. Everyone you email will thank you by actually reading your email once you put the principles into practice, which you will."

—ERIKA HALL, cofounder of Mule Design Studio; author of *Just Enough Research* and *Conversational Design*

"Ashley and Dayana know well-crafted email is like all successful marketing—it builds and maintains trusting relationships with audiences and offers them value, inspiring them to exchange value in return. Ashley and Dayana will teach you everything you need to learn about unleashing the power of this channel. You'll be astonished by the outcomes when you put their ideas to work."

—TERRY FLANNERY, CASE executive vice president and COO; author of *How to Market a University*

"Need a tactical and practical guide to your email? This book does the job, and then some. Take a moment to invest in yourself and your organization's email with this phenomenal read."

—**LYNNE WESTER,** founder and principal, Donor Relations Group; cohost of the #1 fundraising podcast, *Fundraising is Funny*

"This is the best book I've read on email marketing. Drawing from decades of their own success, Ashley and Dayana reveal everything they know about how to put email to work for your unique organization. *Mailed It!* is an invaluable resource for marketers everywhere!"

—**KRISTINA HALVORSON,** owner of Brain Traffic; author of *Content Strategy for the Web*; host of *The Content Strategy Podcast*; executive producer of Button

A GUIDE TO CRAFTING EMAILS THAT BUILD
RELATIONSHIPS AND GET RESULTS

ASHLEY BUDD and DAYANA KIBILDS

RIVER GROVE
BOOKS

Published by River Grove Books
Austin, TX
www.rivergrovebooks.com

Distributed by River Grove Books

Design and composition by Greenleaf Book Group
Cover design by Ashley Budd

Publisher's Cataloging-in-Publication data is available.

Print ISBN: 978-1-63299-865-1

eBook ISBN: 978-1-63299-866-8

First Edition

To our readers.
We hope this book finds you well.

CONTENTS

INTRODUCTION

Think back to how it felt to wake up on your birthday and get exactly the gift you wished for.

Or the first time you got a Valentine from someone who wasn't in your immediate friend group at school.

Or the feeling of winning a game of chance, like a raffle or Bingo.

Or the lucky shock of finding a $50 bill discarded on the street.

Excitement. Incredulity. Unfiltered joy. I can't believe this is happening to me.

That's how getting an email used to feel, too. But it doesn't anymore. And that's why the world needs this book. Let's write better emails.

―

Hi! Welcome to our book. We're probably too excited that you're here, so we will rely on our editor to dial us back.

We are Dayana and Ashley. We met at Cornell University, where we worked on digital engagement and fundraising strategies amid peak digital disruption. Social media changed the way we connected, and technology was, for the first time, in the palm of our hands.

We're millennial women, which means we're digital natives. Online communication comes naturally to us. We've made careers out of optimizing it for nonprofits and universities. We know email can be used for good.

But honestly, most email suuuuuuucks. When you think of your email inbox, what words come to mind? We've asked hundreds of marketers this question, and the top responses are: overwhelming, time-suck, and ugh. The inbox is not a pleasant place to be. Most emails are way too long. They are unclear and lack a communication strategy. So that's why we're here—to make emails better and the time spent reading them enjoyable.

OUR EMAIL ORIGIN STORY

As millennials with early adopter tendencies, we made our careers by being the first to take digital seriously at our respective jobs in the early 2000s. Ashley now runs a very successful email marketing operation in advancement at Cornell University, raising millions of dollars a year for deserving students and critical research. Dayana has been getting people to read and act on email since 2009, from simple B2B campaigns to complex journeys for high school students.

We both have a soft spot for email and want it to stop being the ugly duckling of your marketing mix. And we thought it would be cute to explain exactly where that soft spot comes from.

Dayana

I've had an email address since 1995, when I was 10 years old and my family got our first free AOL CD at a Publix in Florida. I never realized it until this very moment—writing this introduction—that since then, email has been a really important channel in my life. When I was 15 years old, my family moved to Mexico City. I made my first Hotmail email address to stay in touch with my friends in Florida. When I was 18 years old, I applied to a university in Germany through an email with a bunch of attachments, and my acceptance was a simple reply from my advisor. I moved to Germany on my own when I was 18. This was before social media, so email was the only way I communicated with the three very important people in my life. My dad, who emailed me every day. My best friend, with whom I exchanged weekly updates about the boys in our life. And the very occasional, very in-depth email from "the one who got away" in high school, who is now my partner of 16 years.

Email back then was how I kept and nourished the most important relationships in my life.

Fast forward to my first serious job in 2009. I worked at a Mexican sales subsidiary of a company headquartered in Germany. We sold original German car parts wholesale to the Mexican aftermarket, naturally with a price premium compared to imitation products. I realized quickly we needed to generate demand from the end user . . . the car owners who wanted to replace their headlight bulbs with the original, or the mechanics who wanted to use sensors they could trust. So, I launched a monthly newsletter—and unknowingly, the email marketing part of my career began. We were lucky back then, people actually paid attention because email wasn't as popular as it is now.

Later, I moved again, this time as the trailing spouse, relocating to Penn State University for my husband to start his PhD. In my starting roles at Penn State, email was a part of my role but not the focus. It became the focus when I began leading the customer relationship management (CRM) team for undergraduate recruitment. I realized email was chaos, and I wanted to make it not chaos.

My first email initiative got more people to sign up for our open houses than ever before, and it got 20 different campuses to coordinate on a single strategy, also like never before. From there I went to Cornell University, where annual giving emails were my entire role. I got to play around with Giving Day emails too. For the first time, my emails *made money!* That's when I realized I knew things about email I could share with other folks. I noticed that the work I had been doing with email to that point had gotten results. I got people to open them. I got people to read them. I got people to take action. I wanted to turn my intuition into something anyone could do.

So, with Ashley's encouragement, I started speaking at conferences. My first conference talk was about coordinating email strategy with stakeholders. It won an award. I then moved to Canada and started working in undergraduate recruitment at Western University. The first thing I did was overhaul our email strategy. I saw open rates I couldn't believe, in the 80% to 90% range. We blew our yield conversion (that's when students accept an offer of admission) record out of the water. This wasn't due to email alone, but email was a huge part of our recruitment strategy, and it was giving major results. That's when I started running trainings and workshops on how to write better emails based on the stuff I had tried and tested myself. And ever since, the feedback I get time and time again is: What I teach works.

Ashley

My earliest memories of email are from my first job after college. I went to school for painting and earned a bachelor of fine arts in 2007. My academic career up to that point had very little to do with electronic correspondence. After graduating, the reality of opening my own studio with a stack of private school loans hit hard. As a student, I worked in the undergraduate admissions office as a tour guide, and I saw an opportunity to keep working for the university. I applied to a master's program in Communication and Media Technology, and the admissions office kept me employed as a graduate assistant.

Soon I was hired full-time as an admissions counselor. My master's was paid for by the university, and I settled into my first job as a professional. I remember putting on dress clothes for work (I'm not doing that anymore) and going into an office every day (not doing that either.) I would sit down at my desk with my office-issued Blackberry Pearl and turn on my desktop computer.

I'd take a whole fifteen minutes or so to read through all of my emails. All twelve of them. I'd pore over each one, taking in every detail and clicking every link. I'd respond to one or two that needed my attention and then go on with my day. The email newsletters looked like the front page of newspapers with a masthead, issue date, and carefully designed boxes for each little story to fit in. So many newsletters still look like this today.

Not long after starting my admissions counselor role, I was tapped to produce the admissions office emails to prospective students and parents. I was an obvious choice for the job—I was 22. I knew my way around the software, not because I had used it before but because I'd had my hands on software programs my entire life. I taught myself HTML and found immense satisfaction in writing, designing, and debugging emails. They were important communications and I was at the center of them.

Once social media became mainstream, my focus shifted. Like Dayana, I've always been an early adopter of new technology and this was no different. My love for email writing morphed into an obsession with marketing. I took every marketing course available at the university. I became enthralled with the science of persuasion and influence. *How do I get people to take action? How do I get results?*

My whole career has a digital throughline, and prior to that my passions were always a form of communication: art, music, writing—expressions to make people feel good and bring enjoyment into their lives. That's why I'm here. To show you how to make this mess of an email space enjoyable and to share my science-based insights that reveal why it works.

But, loving email isn't enough for you to trust us. Instead, we thought we'd share quotes from marketers who have gone to our talks and trainings, and the results they've seen after applying the tips you'll read in this book.

From a marketing and communications director at a university:

"I was so inspired by the workshop Ashley and Dayana delivered. I found myself nodding the whole time and saying to myself, 'Amen!' Such valuable and approachable content."

From a writer at a big state school:

"We had a very long, complicated email we were sending out. We were trying to cover several issues and deadlines in one email. We used your tips and had people writing to thank us for the clear information!"

From a fundraiser trying to get visits with donors:

"I just wanted to reach out to you and let you know that I've had TREMENDOUS success using your suggestions! My response rate has tripled! Can't thank you enough."

From a conference talk attendee:

"Knowing I can apply these techniques to our quarterly email is fantastic! I have struggled to get a format that I felt would have the most impact, now I know what to do. Also, I now have expert advice to back me up when I'm making a case for simple language. Thank you!!"

From a workshop attendee:

"I immediately took a 'monster' email and broke it down into four separate emails to be sent when more relevant and timely. I plan to do that with more of our emails. I also plan to create a master email schedule for our office."

WHO ARE YOU?

One of the very first things we did at the start of this book project was identify exactly who we were writing for. You. Let us tell you how we see you.

You are at an inflection point in your career, maybe in your first or second role. We see you at a mission-driven organization, in education, government, or nonprofit. Email is a significant part of your job—not just to communicate with your colleagues or stakeholders, but to achieve your organization's goals. You use email to reach readers and to make things happen, like increasing donations, getting people to sign up for events, or enrolling a cohort of students.

But, there is no handbook. You inherited a handful of templates or you are going off your own instinct. You're writing and sending emails the same way it's always been done before. No one has taught you how to plan emails or how to write emails, and you're doing the very best you can. Sometimes your emails work just fine, other times you can't figure out why people aren't reading them. You've said once or twice "people don't read our emails anymore" because you keep getting questions from your readers about something you clearly included, or because you're just not seeing the metrics and results you expect.

This book will help. You'll notice this book is foundational, but it's not basic. It assumes that you have been working with email for one to two years already, and that you have a robust understanding of what your organization is trying to accomplish through email. We expect you to be used to writing emails, and we expect you to be familiar with basic email terminology.

If you are a bit more advanced, we expect you to understand how customer relationship management software (CRM) manages information, how dynamic content can be programmed, and how to understand basic email performance metrics.

There's a bonus too. This book is primarily written to help you get your audiences to do things to meet your organization's goals. But it will also help with your day-to-day communication with your colleagues. After you read this book, you'll never again struggle with Julie from purchasing or Cameron from IT not reading your emails.

WE THINK OUR BOOK IS SPECIAL

This book is different from other email marketing books. Most of those are sales-oriented books whose priority is to get leads—prospective customers—closer to purchase. No shade to that objective, but this is a very different type of email book.

We think email is intimate. We don't believe in trickery. We respect our email readers and we want their trust. We wanted to create a book that is about the relationships you build and maintain with your readers, offering them value and getting value in return.

For that same reason, this book is foundational. It isn't about the latest and greatest, newest, most innovative email trends out there. For that, we recommend litmus.com, hubspot.com, and reallygood emails.com. This book is for people who want to invest in email as a serious part of their marketing mix (rather than as an afterthought), who want to build trusting relationships with their readers, and who want to set up a solid foundation that works. Once you have those, the newest trends and innovations will be your cherry on top.

Our editor asked us, Why are you writing this book now? Why not three years ago, why not three years from now?

Three years ago was in the middle of the COVID-19 pandemic, so we were each trying to survive with our respective strong-willed, scary-smart toddlers at home. But we don't think that's what our editor meant. Professionally, three years ago, we were just starting to put together the pieces of all the email knowledge we had separately. In 2022, we realized—while drinking a glass of wine and eating an entire tray of cheese at the CASE Summer Institute for Communications & Marketing volunteer faculty lobby—that together, we had enough content to write a book. And so we did.

Once we started writing, it felt urgent. It felt urgent because we know email can help marketers achieve their goals. We saw our friends who manage social media struggle to keep up with algorithm changes, new platforms, the death of organic reach, and the loss of Twitter. We see Google Search results riddled with irrelevant ads and websites that put the burden on the visitor to figure out what information applies to them. Through all this, email remains strong and steady—but so many marketers don't know how to leverage its power. We think this book is important now because we think it's a solution for you to maintain your relationship with your readers through uncertainty and change, and the more marketers learn how to do email better, the better email will work for everyone.

WHAT'S IN THE BOOK

This is what you can expect from this lovely little book of ours:

- In chapters 1 and 2 we explain why email matters and the psychology behind what makes a good email. Use these two chapters to impress your boss with your email smarts.

- In chapters 3 and 4 we explain how to build an audience and the different types of strategies you can create to nurture your relationship with them and work toward your marketing goals.

- Chapters 5 and 6 are the most tactical. We get very specific with how you need to write and structure your emails so your readers get your point quickly. If you read nothing else in this book, read these two chapters. They are life changing.

- In chapter 7 we show you how to manage multiple stakeholders, whether strategizing or writing. You're welcome.

- Chapter 8 shows you how to measure your success. Spoiler: You get to decide how you measure your success.

- And in chapter 9 we show you how to run an effective email operation, down to the people and tools you need to make it happen.

When all is said and done, here's a list of all the things we hope you learn (use this as a checklist, we *know* you like crossing things off 😊):

- How readers' brains make decisions
- How to craft effective email strategies based on trust
- How a reader's eyes consume information quickly
- How to write content so that your reader opens the email and gets your point

- How to format and lay out an email so it can be scanned in 2 seconds or less

- How to get a reader to take action

- How to track your success

- How to set up and run an efficient and effective email operation

YOUR PROMISE TO US

We wrote this book because we want better email for everyone. We're sharing what has worked for us because we want it to work for you too.

What's in this book is powerful. You'll see it in your open rates and click-throughs. And because of that, we need you to promise us this: You will use your new powers for good.

We don't believe in tricking our audiences into opening something that isn't relevant. We don't believe in enticing them to click on something that's not useful. Respecting your readers is the most foundational premise of this book. Is this a manifesto? Let's make it one.

We will create value. We will make people feel good. If that's what you want too—well, friend, let's freaking go.

Chapter 1

WHY EMAIL?

Not everyone loves email as much as we do, but everybody uses it. For most, it's a primary communication tool and part of our everyday personal and professional lives. The first email was sent in 1971! This technology has survived over half a century because of a few unique benefits compared to other communication channels.

Today, email serves as an essential utility. It's the contemporary version of a paper trail. Email is used for things like keeping a correspondence record, authenticating your identity, receiving bill statements, and other important notifications. Compared to its digital contemporaries, email is considered a more professional communication channel than chats, text messaging, and social media.

Email is one of the most widely available communication channels we have. Almost everyone has an email address, email is easy to use, and your email account is accessible from anywhere in the world from many popular devices, including computers, mobile phones, and wearable technology.

BENEFITS OF EMAIL

Email is a convenient tool for many things. You can use email to send invitations or share information. It can be entertaining. Email is good for getting people to take action. It's also good for keeping in touch with the people or organizations you care about. Of course, you can do all these things through other channels, like mail, phone, or advertising, but the benefits and unique features of email have given this channel staying power.

We gravitate to email as a primary communication channel because it is efficient. Consider how long it takes to send a message through the postal mail or how difficult it might be to relay detailed information through a phone call.

Email is fast, practically instantaneous, and reliable. When you need to send files, email offers the flexibility of linking to resources or sending attachments. The attachments can't get lost like some of your packages do. And, emails serve as an official record of correspondence too.

Email is asynchronous, unlike phone calls or in-person meetings, allowing us to communicate at different times, making it a convenient option for people with busy schedules or living in different time zones. In addition, an email's global reach is valuable for businesses and maintaining personal connections worldwide. A 2020 survey of marketers found that for every US dollar invested in email marketing, brands earned $36.[1] This was even higher in retail, ecommerce, and the consumer goods sector.

UNIQUE FEATURES OF EMAIL

The software we use to send and receive emails includes features that stand out among other digital communication channels. The email inbox has a unique design.

---

1   Dencheva, Valentina. "Email marketing return on investment (ROI) in selected industries according to marketers worldwide as of June 2020." *Statista* March 15 (2023). https://www.statista.com/statistics/804656/email-roi-perception/.

Each email provides information about who it's from, the subject, and a preview of the contents. These components are viewable "outside" the email before you even open it. Inside the email, you can have a lot more (sometimes too much) information. In the inbox, you can organize emails to fit your preferences. You can sort, filter, and tag communications, making it easier to manage a large volume.

Email offers more flexible formats than digital communication channels like social media and text messaging. Emails also have a longer lifespan. They can stay in your inbox forever, and they can be forwarded or shared with other people. Even though emails live on platforms hosted through service providers, email is considered an owned media channel.

Owned media refers to physical or digital channels that your organization has complete control over. That means you control who is on your email list and when your messages will be delivered compared to social or paid media channels that rely on an algorithm-driven news feed or advertising placement.

TODAY'S EMAIL LANDSCAPE

Ray Tomlinson sent the first email over fifty years ago when he created ARPANET's networked electronic mail system. The project was part of the US Department of Defense communication technology research and laid the groundwork for the creation of the internet. In an interview with *The Verge* in 2012, Tomlinson said, "There was no really good way to leave messages for people. The telephone worked up to a point, but someone had to be there to receive the call. ... So everyone latched onto the idea that you could leave messages on the computer."[2]

Email hit the mainstream in the early 1990s. Since then, the email evolution has been drastic. That first email in 1971 didn't look like the

---

2   Hicks, Jesse. "Ray Tomlinson, the inventor of email: 'I see email being used, by and large, exactly the way I envisioned.'" *The Verge* May 2 (2012). https://www.theverge. com/2012/5/2/2991486/ray-tomlinson-email-inventor-interview-i-see-email-being-used.

email you might have sent today. Likewise, the emails we see now look very different than they did even in the early 2000s. Emails adopted HTML and began to look more like websites. They've become responsive to our mobile devices and they've introduced interactivity and dynamic content.

MORE EMAILS THAN EVER

If you feel like you're getting more emails than ever, it is because you are! The volume of emails has increased dramatically. The amount of outbound communication from businesses has increased, and the amount of personal email you receive is likely to have increased too. In 2022, there were an estimated 333 billion emails sent and received daily around the world. This figure is projected to increase to 392.5 billion daily emails by 2026.[3]

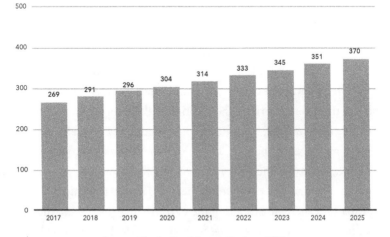

Number of sent and received emails per day worldwide from 2017 to 2025 (in billions)

Source: The Radicati Group, Statista, 2023

---

3   Ceci, Laura. "Number of sent and received emails per day worldwide from 2017 to 2026." *Statista* August 22 (2023). https://www.statista.com/statistics/456500/daily-number-of-e-mails-worldwide/.

As a result, managing communication in your inbox is very different than it once was. And because the volume has increased, inbox behaviors aren't the only ones that have changed. A decade ago, you spent much more time reviewing each email. That time has eroded simply because of how many emails are received daily.

Along with an increase in communication volume, there has also been an increase in concerns around privacy and security. Email is vulnerable to hacking and phishing attacks, and now more people know the risks of sharing sensitive information over email. As a result, email service providers and businesses have had to take steps to protect user data and provide more secure paths for communication.

TECHNOLOGY INNOVATIONS

Email technology from service providers has gotten more sophisticated, enabling more exciting designs and animations. Today, this technology has advanced features like filters, reminders, and scheduling tools that support organization and productivity.

Many email service providers will presort your emails for you. Innovations like the junk folder weren't part of our world when email communication started. Now, not only is there a junk bin, but people can sort messages by priority flags or in archival folders. And tools can sort your email by what they think is important to you, based on your past behaviors and other algorithmic hunches. Providers can flag emails that are corporate promotions, junk, and spam.

As devices got smaller, email technology became mobile-friendly. Now you can access your emails on the go, and as a result, email is consumed in different contexts. People check their email while they're commuting, out for a walk, and in other public spaces—emails designed for the person on the go perform well. If an email is designed with a busy person in mind, it will be easy to read quickly and even easier to consume by someone who can take their time. Designs must be readable on smaller screens and should be simple enough to load quickly on slower data connections.

MARKETING INNOVATIONS

Email marketing has become more sophisticated. For example, businesses are using data-driven personalization techniques to customize messages. These tactics range from simple to complex, from using a person's name in a subject line to creating completely dynamic content throughout the body of an email. Personalization can also involve narrowing your audience lists to speak more directly to one group or sending targeted follow-ups based on individual interests or behaviors (more on audiences and segmenting in chapter 3).

In the same space, automation tools have become more prevalent. Automation enables businesses to send triggered emails that follow specific actions. For example, a newsletter writer sends a welcome email automatically to a new subscriber, or an online retailer uses automation to send a reminder email whenever someone abandons a shopping cart transaction. Both emails recognize an action that was taken and help bring the reader or customer along to the next step in their journey. Emails that anticipate needs build trust between the reader and sender and lead to better email performance.

AI AND EMAIL

Artificial intelligence is changing the way we approach a lot of everyday tasks. Email service providers have been offering AI-enabled assistance for a while now. Outlook 365 introduced Cortana broadly during the pandemic to help customers save time and focus attention. The product now offers a conversational AI that lets users ask the assistant to schedule meetings, compose emails, manage their calendar and inbox, and find information. Similarly, other large email service providers like Gmail have been recommending follow-up actions and suggesting how to craft email responses.

As AI infiltrates more of these workflows, we can expect greater efficiencies. And with efficiency comes the ability to produce a greater email volume more quickly. AI will also assist in how we receive and filter emails. It will improve the email experience by helping us prioritize the messages we want to receive and present them to us when we want to read them.

HOW DO PEOPLE USE EMAIL?

People interact with their inbox based on how much email they get. The average person receives more than 100 emails each day. Because the hours in a day are fixed, as the volume of incoming email increases, the amount of time we can spend on each email decreases. In fact, we've been seeing that decrease on time spent reading email over the last few years.

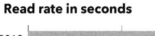

Read rate in seconds

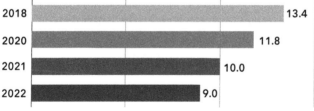

Year	Seconds
2018	13.4
2020	11.8
2021	10.0
2022	9.0

Source: Litmus Email Engagement Report, 2022

Readers who need to consume more than 100 emails each day often adopt these reading habits:

- Using preset inbox filters
- Deleting emails without opening them
- Skimming emails rather than reading them
- Flagging emails for later follow-ups

How do we build effective communication in this landscape? There are two principles to consider. (1) Communication = message received. If someone doesn't get our message because they don't open or read it, we haven't completed our task. (2) Humans process information in a predictable pattern.

As marketers, we strive for long-lasting relationships built on short-term campaigns that take people on a journey. When we want readers to complete a specific task for us, such as registering for an upcoming event, the sequence of our messages needs to be carefully crafted to compel someone to act. Many marketing models address this psychology. The most popular is the AIDA model, referred to as the purchase funnel, the marketing funnel, or the sales funnel. AIDA stands for awareness, interest, desire, and action. The model illustrates a theoretical customer journey from getting the customer's attention to the point of sale. The concept is used to highlight steps that are often ignored by marketers but are essential to meeting customer needs. We'll refer to this phenomenon as the psychology of influence—a human-centered approach that influences reader decisions.

Throughout this book, we'll apply the psychology of influence to email and demonstrate tactics to help you communicate effectively with your readers at each step of their journey.

THE PSYCHOLOGY OF INFLUENCE

The psychology of influence breaks down how our brains work in decision-making processes. Research shows it's easier for readers to make decisions when they are primed with information that supports the action they are about to take. For example, a reader is more likely to purchase a product if they have previous knowledge of it and understand the benefits than if they are being introduced to it for the first time.

There are four steps in this psychological framework.

The first step is **awareness**. Someone must know that you, your organization, or your specific marketing campaign exists. Without the awareness that you're doing something, how can anyone be compelled to take action?

The second step is **nurture**. Once your audience knows what you're up to, you can connect the dots for them. Use language and storytelling to help them understand why your campaign is important and how they fit into it.

The third step is **action**. They now have all the information they need. Asking your reader to take action is the easy part. You've already made them aware of your campaign, and they believe it matters to them. The sender's objective at this step is to provide super clear and easy steps for readers to follow and do what you want them to do.

The last step is **stewardship**. Once your reader has taken action, reward them with follow-up. Show your gratitude and report back on the campaign's results. This communication step is key to solidifying an ongoing relationship, building trust, and setting them up for the next call-to-action coming their way. Stewardship is a big piece missing from the AIDA model.

This psychology is an important context for understanding audience behaviors. If your email is for action, you might be asking why we suggest spending so much time raising awareness and nurturing relationships before asking the reader to do something. The answer is this is simply how our brains work.

When we're given all the information we need to make a decision, we're primed to take action. These first steps in the communication process provide clarity. Clarity should be part of your email writing philosophy. Clarity is why, when things are designed well, people want to interact with them. In most cases, your call-to-action has little to do with the merits of your message and everything to do with whether the person understands what you're asking them to do.

Clarity helps us rationalize our decisions. It helps us believe in messages. And people, for better or worse, trust information that is easy to believe.

Key Takeaways

- Email remains a powerful and essential communication tool, with unique benefits such as flexibility, reliability, personalization, and significant return on investment.

- There is more email now than ever before, and less time to read it. This makes it crucial to build relationships, ensure relevance, and write effectively.

- Understanding how our brains make decisions is foundational to crafting effective email strategies.

Chapter 2

WHAT MAKES A GOOD EMAIL?

What is the difference between a good email and a bad email? In a lot of ways, it's subjective. An email could be plain text with terrible formatting, but if it's also a sweet note from your grandmother, you might consider it precious. One way to think about what makes a good email is to consider whether it's an email someone wants to receive.

Marketers and designers use the word *content* as a catch-all for everything we stuff into our emails, websites, and apps. Content can be tested and optimized and can easily fall into the trap of being formulaic instead of creative. As marketers, our creative side often struggles with content development. Marketers want content to fit into perfect boxes. The result is dull creations. To that end, in this book, we do our best to describe our work as an artistic process instead of content creation.

How we label our work is important. You will approach an email suite differently if you are told to provide artwork and creative writing vs. being told to draft email content. Creation of any kind is an artistic expression. It's personal, original, and beautiful. If a reminder to create good content for email dulls your expression, swap the word content for art.

PUT YOUR AUDIENCE FIRST

You get people to read essential emails by having a solid reputation and considering their time. Without these factors, your emails can be easily discarded—like physical junk mail that goes directly from your mailbox to the trash bin. If you want someone to read your whole email, consider how much time they have to spend on it. Good email is about creating a good experience.

Saying things with fewer words respects the reader and enhances their experience. When you need to deliver a lot of information, keep the details hosted elsewhere, like on your website or in a supporting document. **Your email is a conversation vehicle, not the place for a manifesto.** Instead, use an email to set up your manifesto and invite people to visit your website for more.

Good emails always respect the reader. In an environment where email volume is increasing, every moment a reader spends in the email inbox is calculated. Let's say you receive 100 emails daily, and you have two whole hours of your day dedicated to reading and responding to emails. That means you could spend just over one minute on each email correspondence.

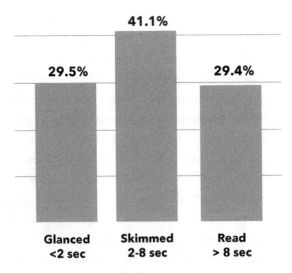

Source: Litmus Email Engagement Report, 2022

That timing is extremely generous. In reality, most readers only dedicate a few seconds to their emails. In 2022, Litmus found that 30% of emails, on average, are looked at for less than 2 seconds, 41% are looked at for between 2–8 seconds, and only 29% are looked at for more than 8 seconds. Keeping your emails concise respects the reader's time and gives you a much higher chance that your message will be received.

CALLS-TO-ACTION

Just like your essential messaging, calls-to-action (CTAs) work when they are clear and brief and have next steps laid out that are easy to complete. When you are asking someone to do something, you need to respect their time and understand the context in which they are receiving your email. For someone to take action, they need to have information about what you are asking them to do and understand why their action matters.

If you don't want to be ignored, invest in the relationship with your reader. Be helpful and considerate and deliver valuable information regularly. By building a program that consistently delivers good emails over time, you will create good reading habits among your subscribers.

CHOOSING THE RIGHT CTA

When writing a call-to-action (CTA) message, clearly state what you want the reader to do. Large buttons with clear language help readers understand and focus on your task.

For example, your organization has just released new research that will improve the well-being of the community members it serves. Great news! What's the call-to-action? Spoiler alert: It's not "Learn more."

Asking someone to read or learn more about your program will not drive someone to act. In this example, the sender needs the reader to read and learn. But what they are really after is a bigger action. The organization wants them to share this important research with more people and implement the findings in their community. This calls for a stronger call-to-action than reading or learning. Clearer calls-to-action are "Share these findings" or "Make lives better."

Sometimes your call-to-action is to gather feedback or ask for advice. If you want people to reply to your message, make sure they know you're looking for a reply. If you want someone to forward your email to friends, tell them, and don't be afraid to be specific. It's easy to get cute about email copy and forget to be clear.

STANDING OUT IN THE INBOX

Capturing attention is a critical skill for email marketers. This book is not about gimmicks. Gimmicks can capture attention once or twice. The organizations that keep our attention are the ones we trust and adore most. Still, to stand out, you need to be there in the first place. Sending quality emails helps you land in the inbox instead of junk.

FROM NAMES AND SUBJECT LINES

Let's start with the landscape of the modern email inbox. Readers follow a simple pattern each time they open their email. The first thing they do is look for From names they recognize. Next, they will scan email subject lines. Based on what is displayed here, decisions about what gets opened and what gets trashed happen in seconds.

Include a recognizable name for your reader to spot when they first glance through their inbox. If the individual sending the email is unknown, clearly display the organization they represent.

"From" names are read first, but subject lines are the next place to stand out. You can draw attention to your email by being clear about what's inside your email and using emojis that add context. Clear doesn't mean you can't be fun. The more you build a relationship with your readers, the more fun you can be.

Remember, communication = message received. If you need to communicate that your next Open House is on March 15, say that in your subject line. Don't hide this message in the body of the email. If most people read the subject line and don't open your email, your message will still be received. Communication success! If they need to take an action, put it in the subject line. You could say, "Register for the March 15 Open House." Clear From names and subject lines will help your reader receive your message in seconds and understand what you are asking them to do next. More on this in chapter 6.

TRUSTWORTHY EMAIL

The key to a good relationship with your readers is trust. If they trust you to send messages they want, they will open and read your emails even if they aren't exactly sure what they are expecting to receive from you. Trust like that takes time to build. You need to prove that you are an authentic, honest communicator. You need to prove that you care about the person on the other side of the communication. And you need to be realistic about what you're asking someone else to do.

This brings us to our favorite trust model—the Trust Triangle. According to leadership experts Frances Frei and Anne Morriss, trust has three core drivers. You can build trust by emphasizing authenticity, empathy, and logic in your communication. In the May–June 2020 issue of the *Harvard Business Review* magazine, Frei and Morriss explain people are more likely to trust you when they believe they are interacting with the real you (authenticity), when they believe you care about them (empathy), and when they can follow your judgment and believe in your ability to make good decisions (logic). They say when trust is lost, the reason can be traced back to a breakdown in one of these core drivers.[4]

---

4   Frei, Frances X. and Morriss, Anne. "Begin with Trust." *Harvard Business Review* May–June (2020). https://hbr.org/2020/05/begin-with-trust.

THE TRUST TRIANGLE

To leverage the Trust Triangle—authenticity, empathy, and logic—as a writer, you need to meet the readers' needs in all these areas. If trust in the email sender is weak, it might be that one point of your triangle is not as strong as the others. Frei and Morriss call this a "wobbly triangle." Understanding where you wobble will help you pick an area to improve.

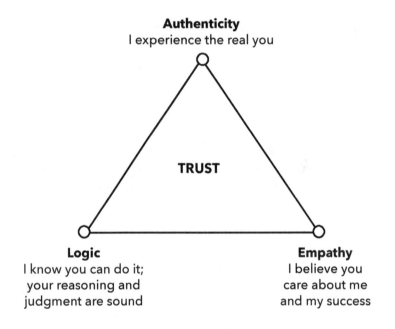

Authenticity
I experience the real you

TRUST

Logic
I know you can do it;
your reasoning and
judgment are sound

Empathy
I believe you
care about me
and my success

From "Begin with Trust" by Frances Frei and Anne Morriss,
Harvard Business Review May-June 2020

Authenticity

At the top of the triangle is authenticity. Authenticity is an honesty test. Are you telling the truth? Are you keeping it real? Or has your writing become clouded with formalities, bad writing habits, and what you think you should say rather than what you want to say and what your audience needs to hear? If a reader can poke holes in your messaging, they will.

Being authentic often means being vulnerable. Not all truths are easy to swallow. If you represent an organization, share the reality of the business. Show a little bit of what is happening behind the scenes. Talk about the people who make your organization great. Share your goals. Organizations with a checkered past are more authentic when they recognize where they once were as they grow and move forward.

If you represent yourself, you should lean into the pieces of yourself that make you unique and human. Even if these aspects of yourself seem off-topic, showing a little bit of realness can bring the reader closer to you, and this builds trust.

Remember, authenticity means keeping it real. So, don't describe something as exciting when it's not. Don't say something will be quick if it takes more than a few minutes. Don't lead with how great your organization is without acknowledging the parts of your organization that need improvement.

Empathy

The second point on the triangle is empathy. Organizations learned many lessons about empathy during the pandemic: how to connect with people where they are, be sensitive to the complexity of life and family, and provide value in innovative ways. And it seems they forgot all of them! During the pandemic, we were very concerned about others. We took the time to understand what state of mind people would be in when they received our messages. Our messaging changed as a result. We crafted language more carefully, and we had a genuine concern for our readers.

Empathy builds trust. Empathetic writers are invested in their readers' success. They consider what value they are providing to a reader in every email message. Are you sharing helpful information? Are you making them smile? Are you offering them an experience that will make them feel good? Oftentimes, organizations are laser-focused on their own success and leave the audience out of it.

If we lay out our goals and simply hope our readers will join in, we're missing a critical piece. We must show them how our goals are connected to their own and where mutual benefit exists. When we're empathic, when our readers know we're invested in their success, we build trust.

There is such a thing as too much information. People, on average, take 2 seconds to skim an email. For those who are more invested, that skim can last up to 8 seconds. If you've captured attention, now you have a reader. Readers can only commit a fixed amount of time to reading and responding to each email they receive. So treat their time as being as precious as your own.

Logic

The last point on the triangle is logic. Your readers need to be able to follow you. They need to know why you're communicating with them and what you are asking them to do, and they need clear steps to follow to complete each action. You can have great authentic and empathetic messaging and then lose your reader to confusing calls-to-action.

When your message is logical and clear, the reader can follow your motives and instructions without questioning them. However, each time we do something that makes a reader question us, we lose them.

In an email, readers are making split-second decisions. Do I need this email? Should I keep reading? Should I click through to see what's next? Many of these decisions are made subconsciously based on prior experiences. When readers have trust in you as the sender, they are more likely to develop consistent reading and click-through habits.

Consistency is an important part of your email marketing strategy. When you deliver quality emails on a reliable schedule you build trust. Support what you're saying with evidence, so the reader has confidence that what you're saying is true. You can do this with data, like facts and figures, stories, or testimonials from others who support what you're trying to communicate. Combine this consistency with simple language and clear calls-to-action,, and now they can follow your logic.

RELEVANT EMAIL

Creating content that is relevant to your reader is critical to a successful email program. You need to reach people at the right time with the right message. This is what it means to be relevant. Ask yourself, what is happening in their life right now, and how is your message showing up? Is it relevant? If it's not, it's more likely to be discarded.

You can develop relevant email messages by really knowing your audience. But when audiences are large and diverse, it can be difficult to decide what might be relevant to everyone. In these cases, tap into universal truths, seasons, national holidays, and aspects of everyday life that are relatable.

For example, each new year sparks something in us to set goals and start new endeavors. You can meet your audience where they are by inserting your organization into the new year mindset. Offer help with goal setting by sharing a simple meditation or reminder about setting achievable goals. You can share your goals, too, connecting the readers' desire to start something new with your inspiration to move your organization forward. Help them see where they fit in during a time of year that makes sense for this kind of engagement.

PERSONAL VS. PERSONALIZED

We believe personal emails are better than impersonal emails. But personal email doesn't mean every message needs to be personalized with custom language and reader-specific calls-to-action,. Simply striking a personal tone with your reader can be enough to make your message feel personal.

A personal tone is friendly. It reveals your sender personality. Sometimes we focus so much on personalizing for others that we forget to have a personality of our own. Let's pretend for a moment that you run a cheeky local bookstore. You could start an email to sub-scribers with Greetings, <insert first name>. Personalized, yes. Or you could start with Greetings, book lover! Personalized? Yes! You know the reader loves books. They are signed up to learn more about them. Repeating the reader's first name back is easy. Calling on part of their identity and one that directly connects to your business is personal and lets you interject your business personality.

Of course, when you can incorporate even more personalized content for individuals, you might see the message performs better. Just remember that it's not always necessary to personalize to be per-sonal. And in this case, personal tone is everything.

DYNAMIC CONTENT

Email programs that leverage dynamic content—messages and images that show up differently depending on who is receiving your email—require a sophisticated infrastructure. Old-school writers might think of this technique like a modern-day mail merge.

A simple form of dynamic content is including someone's name in your subject line or body copy. More complex emails might have whole paragraphs or calls-to-action, that appear dynamically. For example, that email from your favorite retailer that shows you exactly what you were just shopping for. Technically speaking, dynamic con-tent calls on a database and serves individuals with content based on their preferences, behaviors, or other individual traits. This database links to your email content, which is tagged and formatted in a way your email service provider can ingest.

Dynamic content can be used in email newsletters to display sto-ries and offers that people might want based on their profile or past click behavior. For example, a university might show information about the academic program a prospective student has applied to in an email that is sent during decision-making time.

Dynamic content strategies are especially effective for large organizations that have more content to share than they have time available to share it. These organizations need to prioritize what content will appear in each email, and they know that if given the chance, some readers would choose to prioritize what they see differently. The student who applied to a competitive engineering program might want more information about faculty, while a student who applied to an undecided or exploratory program might prioritize information about academic advising.

Dynamic content allows you to leverage a variety of messages in the same email send to get the most relevant content in front of different readers.

ENGAGING YOUR AUDIENCE

Engagement means connection. Engaging content is a good sign of a strong email program, and key engagement metrics to track in emails include clicks and replies to messages. Sometimes engagement can just be reading. Powerful messages are those that compel people to connect with you, whether that's clicking through, replying to, or just reading the emails you've sent.

Your goal for sustained email engagement is to create a habit with your readers. You want them to see your email in their inbox and know what to do with it instantly. When they see your email, you want them to believe there is good content inside for them. You want to create a habit where every email is opened and clicked on. This is why it's worth investing in clickable content. Some people might call it clickbait. We call it the good stuff.

Being creative means making something new and valuable. Good creative content considers value and relevance and puts a new spin on the message each time. Remember, when you're creating, writing, and designing, you're making art. Treat the process as such, and you'll end up with a unique email that connects with your reader.

Coming up with fresh content regularly is possible with a plan. Set aside time for creative content brainstorming and plan far enough ahead that you have the time to create new things. We know how to nail down the right pace for even the most complex organizations. More on this in chapter 4.

Key Takeaways

- Good emails prioritize the reader's time and experience. Respect their time by delivering concise and relevant content that can be consumed in 8 seconds or less. Focus on providing value and meeting their needs to build trust and engagement.

- To build trust with readers, emphasize authenticity, empathy, and logic in your communication. Be honest, genuine, and clear in your messaging to create a strong bond with your audience.

- Think of creating emails as an artistic process, aiming to deliver unique content and build connections. Plan ahead. Strive for relevance by understanding your audience and connecting with universal themes.

Chapter 3

BUILDING AN AUDIENCE

Who gets your emails? Some of you might have audiences already—precious lists of thousands of email addresses that came with the job (lucky ducks!). Some of you probably purchase lists and have the mountainous task of trying to build affinity through cold emailing (we wish we could tell you not to).

And some of you might be trying to grow your lists one email address at a time, through request-for-information forms, event sign-ups, and other data-collection efforts. This chapter will start there—getting the email addresses—and will then show you how to grow and nurture your lists, keep them clean, and use them effectively through segmentation and audience research.

COLLECTING EMAIL ADDRESSES

Building an audience starts with a very important overarching premise: You want to send emails to readers who want to get emails from you. Even though it breaks our hearts a tiny bit, we are realists, and we know this isn't always the case.

So, we think of the ways to collect email addresses in these four categories, and the nature of how you got the email address determines how hard you have to work to build a relationship with the reader.

HOW YOU GOT THE EMAIL ADDRESS	EXAMPLES	LIKELIHOOD THEY WILL BE ENGAGED
Sign up form: They subscribed or requested more information.	• They saw an ad and went to your website to sign up. • They searched online, found you, and signed up.	High
Opt-in: They took an action with you and consented to get further emails from you.	• They signed up for an event. • They purchased something. • They downloaded something from your website.	Medium
Referral: Someone referred them to you.	• A person close to them forwarded your email or sent them your subscription page.	Medium
Purchased list: You got their email without their knowledge.	• You purchased email addresses. • You sponsored an event and got an attendee list.	Low

Let's talk about some best practices to set you up for success with each of these mechanisms.

SIGN-UP FORM

A sign-up form somewhere on your website is a must, especially if you are running other awareness efforts like advertising in your marketing mix. But, what should your sign-up form include?

Ask for the Data You Are Planning to Use

You'll need a valid email address. And what else? Ask for what you're planning to use. Collecting their first and last names can help with database management and email deliverability if you are sending emails through an email marketing tool.

There is no right or wrong number of fields. In 2021, HubSpot found that conversion rates vary depending on the number of fields, but the relationship between the two variables isn't perfectly linear.[5] Too low and you might get disinterested folks or bad data. Too high and folks might abandon the form before they finish or get suspicious about sharing so much data.

Forms convert better with three, four, or five fields, so ask for what you need to start a good relationship with your reader and not more.

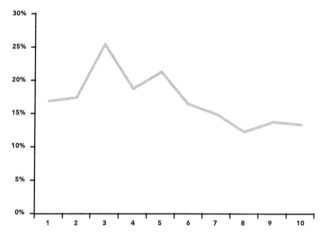

Conversion Rate by Number of Form Fields

Source: HubSpot, Which Types of Form Fields Lower Landing Page Conversions?, 2021

If you want to ask for more than the basics, make sure it's optional. Multi-page or multi-step forms are a great way to get engagement. After they submit the required information, present them with some optional questions they can skip if they want to. Or, set the precedent of them clicking on your emails by sending them a second form in

5   Zarrella, Dan. "Which Types of Form Fields Lower Landing Page Conversions?" *HubSpot* June 11 (2021). https://blog.hubspot.com/blog/tabid/6307/bid/6746/Which-Types-of-Form-Fields-Lower-Landing-Page-Conversions.aspx.

their welcome email (more on welcome emails later in this chapter) where they can give you more details about themselves.

Articulate Your Value Up Front

Let them know exactly what they're getting when they sign up. Use a clear header articulating the value of your content. Have a little fun with the text on your submit button. Set expectations for the frequency and the type of content they can expect from you.

For example, Ashley uses a simple form for her email newsletter "Ashley in Your Inbox."[6] The description says:

> Want to hear from me on a semi-regular basis? I'll send you things I'm excited about—digital strategy, design, work, and life. No agenda. Come and go as you please.

She collects email address, first and last name, and ends the form with a fun call-to-action that says, "Send me letters 🎉."

Get Their Preferences

If you have the technology available, you can ask the reader for their email preferences as they're signing up, reducing the likelihood of unsubscribes or disengagement. Give them the option to set their frequency and content preferences—but only if you can actually modify what you deliver on your end (and only if it is optional and not detracting from them submitting in the first place!).

---

6   Get emails from Ashley https://mailchi.mp/ashleybudd/inbox.

Validate the Data

Validate email addresses at the point of capture using techniques like syntax checks and domain validation. Implement real-time validation during form submissions, for example, checking for an "@" or that common email providers aren't misspelled (gmail vs. gmial) to minimize the chances of collecting bad email data.

OPTING IN

If a reader took an action with you, like attending an event, down-loading something from your website, or purchasing something from you, they are showing interest. It's a good idea to ask if they want to get emails from you because you've clearly already given them something of value.

Common ways to do this are through optional checkboxes on purchase or download forms that say "I agree to receive emails" or asking them during the transaction if it's in person. (We've all been there, right? Every store at the mall does this.)

Here's what's not a good idea: assume they want emails from you because they engaged with you. Not only might it turn them off from your emails, but it might also turn them off from continuing the relationship they started in the first place.

REFERRALS

People forward emails they like. Those in your audience who already like you will be your biggest advocates. Add a link to your sign-up form in the footer of your emails. Encourage readers to forward your email to someone who might enjoy it. And offer an easy way for any-one receiving the email as a forward to sign up for themselves.

PURCHASING LISTS

A common way to increase the size of your audience is to purchase
a list. This might be a direct purchase through a lead vendor, or it
might be acquiring lists as part of sponsorship agreements. In this
case, many of the people on your list don't know they're on your list,
don't know how they got on your list, and probably don't want to be
on your list.

The first email you send to this group should be asking them if
they want to stay on the list. Clearly articulate your value, and who
you best serve, and let them select if they are interested.

MAINTAINING YOUR LISTS

All right, whew, you've done all that work to get email addresses. Now
what? This is where the real work begins.

We won't get into the details of deliverability too much in this
book, because if you pick up what we're putting down you won't
have issues. But, here are the basics: Every email sender out there has
a reputation (as determined by email inbox providers). The better
your sender reputation, the more likely your emails are to land in
your readers' inboxes. Your reputation is made up of a few things:
(1) the frequency and volume of your emails, (2) the reputation of
your IP address and domain, (3) if you've been caught in a spam
trap, and (4) if your readers mark your emails as spam.

Most email service providers will review your sender reputation
monthly. If your emails are getting strong open and click-through
rates, you won't see deliverability issues. If you take time off from
sending or have a streak of low engagement, there might not be
enough data for these tools to go off. In these cases, it's likely you'll
find your mass communication in the junk bin. The best way to avoid
deliverability issues is to maintain and nurture your email lists.

DOUBLE OPT-IN

You've gotten an email like this before, we're sure. They aren't very sexy. Immediately after you sign up for emails, you're told to go to your inbox to confirm. You get a very direct-and-to-the-point-and-usually-quite-ugly email that asks you to confirm your subscription, and once you click, you're on the list. This is called a double opt-in because you basically confirm you want to get emails twice.

This isn't legally required in the United States or Canada (yet), but it is a good practice because implementing a double opt-in process shows respect for your reader and high intent from them. Those readers who double opt-in are much more likely to be and stay engaged with your emails.

THE WELCOME EMAIL

In 2023, the email marketing software provider GetResponse found that welcome emails get three times more opens and clicks than any other emails you send.[7] Why? We'll take a guess. This is the first email you send immediately after your reader has indicated they *want* to get emails from you.

They will never love you more than this moment... so take advantage of it. Use this email to put a smile on their face. Embrace your brand values and voice. Clearly articulate what they can expect from you moving forward. And if you can, give them something of value, like a free download, a discount, or something curated specifically for them that no one else can get.

We believe in welcome emails for purchased names too, but they serve a slightly different purpose. The welcome email for someone who doesn't know how they got on your list should really be a version of the content you're using to convince readers to sign up or opt in. It should look more like your sign-up form than a thank you. Let them

---

7   Leszczynski, Michal. "2023 Email Marketing Benchmarks." *GetResponse*. https://www.getresponse.com/resources/reports/email-marketing-benchmarks#welcome-emails.

know how you got their email address, what preferences they can set, what type of content you will share, and give them an opportunity to say "yes, please" or "no, thank you."

REVIVE THE UNENGAGED

If a reader has not opened your emails in a certain amount of time, you can try to woo them back with a re-engagement campaign.

Think about how you would define "engaged." If you send emails every week, you might consider someone unengaged if they haven't opened an email in three months. If you send an email per month, you might consider someone unengaged if they haven't opened an email in six months.

Send them an email to say you've noticed they haven't been opening or engaging with your content. Be clear in your subject line. How can you serve them better? What content would they like to see? Would they like to pause on getting emails from you? You can offer incentives or special messages to encourage them to re-engage. But, remember to keep it real. Be honest about your email program and what they can expect from you, or they'll be back to ghosting you before you know it.

UNSUBSCRIBING

It is legally required to give your readers the ability to unsubscribe from your emails. In 2024, Gmail will be requiring all senders to make this even easier by mandating the ability to unsubscribe with just one click.[8] This will quickly become the industry expectation (if it isn't already).

Before they go, give them a break.

You can't be sneaky about keeping people on your list; you must

---

8   Kumaran, Neil. "New Gmail protections for a safer, less spammy inbox." *The Keyword* October 3 (2023). https://blog.google/products/gmail/gmail-security-authentication-spam-protection/.

clearly provide an unsubscribe option. But, there is something you can try before it gets to that point. If you know that you are about to ramp up the email volume because of a specific event or campaign, give your readers an option to pause your emails before you push them away completely.

Cornell University's Giving Day is held once a year. In their emails, they add an option to opt-out of Giving Day emails entirely, but they stay subscribed to other emails from Cornell.

> P.S. Is Giving Day not your thing? That's OK too. Opting out of Giving Day emails from the university is quick and easy, and should keep your inbox clear.

Here is another example from Cornell's alumni newsletter around their fiscal year-end. Universities ramp up email volume during this time to meet alumni engagement and fundraising goals, but the readers might not want to be a part of it. Give them an option to pause communications during a preset period, with the clear expectation that they will restart after that.

> Too much in your inbox? Let us know here that you'd like to get less email and we'll remove you from the newsletter until June 30.

REMOVE INACTIVE EMAILS

If you were unsuccessful in reviving your unengaged readers, now it really is time to let them go. Delete or deactivate their emails from your list at least once or twice a year. We recommend this because inactive email addresses hurt your deliverability score, and they also hurt all the other metrics you want to report on to your leadership, like open rates and click rates.

We know it can be hard to do this, especially if you purchased the names. But sending emails to someone who isn't paying attention is only hurting you, we promise. They won't wake up one day and suddenly decide they want to be with you after all. (Why does this section feel like dating advice? Heh.)

CLEAN UP BAD DATA

You'll see the first signs of bad data through emails that bounce. Your email bounce rate is the percentage of emails that did not reach their intended reader due to an email address that is no longer valid or active. These are categorized into "hard" bounces, which are permanent delivery failures, and "soft" bounces, which indicate a temporary issue, such as vacations or a full inbox.

The next place to spot bad email data is through spam complaints. Keep track of the number of readers who report your emails as spam. If someone marks your email as spam, that means your intent to reach them and their desire to be reached are not aligned. You may have "good" email addresses in your audience list, but if these people do not find value in your messaging, they might as well be bad emails.

Manage your data through regular list-cleaning exercises. Remove invalid email addresses, unsubscribed, and inactive subscribers. Use email verification services or software to identify and flag email addresses that are undeliverable or risky. Honor unsubscribe requests quickly to maintain a good sender reputation and comply with email marketing regulations.

AVOIDING SPAM TRAPS

When you hear "spam trap" you might think of something super elaborate, but actually, spam traps look just like regular email addresses. These email addresses are set up by common inbox providers to catch spammers, but it's possible to fall into the trap if you are a legitimate sender who doesn't maintain their list. This chapter shared two easy ways to avoid being caught in a spam trap: (1) use a double-opt-in mechanism—after all, a trap won't double subscribe; and (2) remove inactive recipients from your lists for good.

SEGMENTATION

One of the most common mistakes senders make is sending emails to more people than need to receive them. Especially if the email doesn't apply to them. If you find yourself writing "if this applies to you" in your email copy, that is a very big hint you need to segment your lists further. The more you make this mistake, the more trust you lose, and the less your emails get read over time.

At large organizations, audience list management is a full-time job. And it's worthwhile because, according to HubSpot, segmented emails drive 30% more opens and 50% more click-throughs than unsegmented ones.[9] But, don't get overwhelmed just yet—you don't need dozens of versions of the same email. In fact, 49.3% of marketers report that they create only two to three versions for a single email, and that's about all it takes to see great results from segmentation.[10]

SEGMENTATION VS. DYNAMIC CONTENT

Let's pause here for one second. Segmentation and dynamic content are usually conflated, because in practice they can lead to the same outcome: different sub-groups of readers getting different versions of an email. For clarity, and to keep your email operation manageable, here is how we recommend you use these terms (and implement this work):

- Use segmentation when you want to divide your entire audience into distinct groups because your organization has different messages and unique goals for each group. For example, you want to recruit more international students, or you want to increase donations from recent alumni.

- Use dynamic content when the goals for the group are the same, but you want to serve them with personal or

---

9   Kirsch, Katrina. "The Ultimate List of Email Marketing Stats for 2023." *HubSpot.* December 14 (2023). https://blog.hubspot.com/marketing/email-marketing-stats.

10   Lee, Martyn. "More Than a Name: 10 Ways Marketers Personalize Emails." *Litmus.* May 18 (2022). https://www.litmus.com/blog/more-than-a-name-13-ways-marketers-personalize-emails.

particularly relevant content. For example, a story in
your newsletter that happened in the reader's region or
information about a topic they indicated interest in.

The caveat is if your email tool doesn't allow for dynamic content,
you will have to build segments to achieve personalized content. But
we like to keep these two things conceptually separate to reduce your
mental load of how you need to manage your lists. Remember the lesson from chapter 2, emails don't need to be personalized to be personal.

SEGMENTING BY ATTRIBUTES

Your organization might have specific goals for subsets of your audience based on who or where they are. For example, you might want
to recruit new members locally, or engage a younger demographic, or
promote an event for older adults.

In these cases, it is appropriate to segment by individual attributes,
which include biodemographic information such as age, gender, location, or ethnicity.

However, a huge word of caution. Grab your highlighter because
this is important: Never assume affinity because of identity.

If you know someone's gender or ethnicity, this doesn't mean
you know what they are interested in. Never assume, always ask. Or
you run the risk of causing more harm than good. Tailor content
based on the preferences your reader has indicated or past behavior,
or not at all.

SEGMENTING BY BEHAVIOR

You can make behavioral segmentation very sophisticated if you have
the technology. You could segment based on literally any behavioral
data point you've captured and stored in your CRM. Behavioral
segments are powerful. They also take significant human resource
time to identify and develop strategies for, and can create more work

for content teams. So, only segment based on meaningful insights that will drive your organization's goals.

Example: Moving Readers through a Journey or Funnel

Think about which stages your reader goes through in their relationship with you, and the key milestones that move them from one stage to the next. Each stage could be a separate segment and your emails to them have the goal of moving them to the next stage.

Let's think about this in the context of a prospective student to a college. The stages are prospect, applicant, admit, enrollee. The emails you send to a prospect have the goal to get them to apply. The emails you send them include the content that will convince and prepare them to take that action.

Example: Keeping Readers Engaged

For some of you, your goal isn't necessarily to move someone through a funnel, but to keep them connected to you. Here's an example of how you might segment audience members by engagement type to meet them where they are:

1. Off-the-grid: not responding, might have bad contact information—you might consider a re-engagement campaign with them, and removing them if it doesn't work.

2. Wallflowers: opening emails but not engaging with them— you might want to ask them what type of content they are looking for, or if they need a break from you.

3. Engaged: opening emails and taking action—this is the group you might try new things with, since the trust is there.

4. Super fans: all the opens, clicks, and many replies—keep the frequency and volume high, and possibly even engage them in co-creating content with you!

KNOWING YOUR AUDIENCES

After you've been sending emails for a while, there is so much you can learn from your own data. Start there. You'll quickly see your best send times, the type of content that engages a segment (or doesn't), what your readers click on most. Set aside time at least once a year to dig through your data and create your own audience insights. Use these insights to build your email strategies and segments for the next year.

You can learn even more from doing audience research. We won't dive in deep (we recommend you do!), but here are three of our favorite research methods and what insights you can gain from each:

JOURNEY MAPPING

A journey map is a visual or graphic interpretation of your reader's overall journey and relationship with you, across different channels. This method will help you identify pain points, moments of delight, and opportunities to improve their experience—and how email can play a role in that. To create a journey map, start by choosing a segment or persona. Collect data through interviews, observations, or past behavior. Map out your reader's actions, thoughts, emotions, and pain points on a timeline and identify opportunities for improvement with comments or thought bubbles.

EMPATHY MAPPING

Through an empathy map, marketers gain deeper insight into their reader's psychological and emotional profile. Typically presented in a quadrant, they clearly outline what your reader is thinking, doing, feeling, and seeing or hearing. These are useful to help you create content that emotionally connects to your readers. To create an empathy map, focus on a segment, and carry out interviews or observe behaviors. List your observations as bullet points under each quadrant.

SURVEYS/INTERVIEWS

A self-explanatory one. Reach out to your engaged readers (and those who aren't, too!). Ask what they think of your emails and what they might want to receive from you. You can do this as micro-surveys within your existing email content, as stand-alone surveys you email to them, or as in-person focus groups or one-on-one conversations.

Key Takeaways

- Maintaining a clean email list is a must. You can do this by using double opt-in processes, regularly cleaning up bad data, and removing inactive emails. These practices ensure high deliverability and engagement rates, keep you out of spam traps, and comply with legal requirements for email marketing.

- Segmentation can help you build stronger relationships with your readers. Use segments when you have distinct goals for different groups. Use dynamic content when you want to serve information specific to them. Don't overthink it: You don't need dozens of segments to be effective.

- An email audience is not a list of email addresses you capture and forget. Invest the time in getting to know their patterns and behaviors. Carry out further research to understand the content that will serve readers and build long-term trust.

Chapter 4

EMAIL STRATEGIES

This book is full of email tactics—practical how-tos that get results. But the best email programs are thoughtful and aligned with business goals. These programs are strategic. Your email strategy informs what tactics you'll want to use. This chapter will help you design an email strategy and set you on the path to use the right tactics. At the end of this chapter, we'll give examples of strategies and tactics for email newsletters, marketing funnels, interpersonal emails, and more.

Your email strategy defines your program. Depending on how complex your organization is, you could have a formal documented strategic plan, or you could have a one-line strategy statement that guides your work.

The email strategy for Cornell University's division of alumni affairs and development aligns with an alumni strategic plan, which incorporates alumni needs with operational imperatives like streamlining communication. A one-line email strategy for another alumni organization might be:

Send emails that make alumni smile and stay connected to the institution.

Some tactics for a strategic email program might include:

- Deliver an engaging newsletter and single call-to-action email every week.

- Segment audiences based on life stage and demonstrated interests.

EMAIL STRATEGY FRAMEWORKS

Your strategy is the high-level plan to achieve your long-term goals. You can decide to present it simply or in great detail. Just don't skip it.

It's helpful for teams to have short, clear strategic guides to reference. As you build from your strategy and start to make tactical decisions, you can add to your strategy document. The result is an operational plan. In this documentation, you can include important information about your audience, brand guidelines, benchmarking metrics, and exemplary emails and other marketing pieces.

More detailed strategy documents might include the organization's overall direction and competitive positioning, choices about resource allocation, target markets, differentiation, and value.

Strategy documents provide a framework for decision-making. Email strategies aim to answer the questions of "What are we sending?" and "Why are we sending it?"

GUIDING PRINCIPLES

Creating an email program can feel like a monumental task. Having a solid strategy can make you feel a whole lot better. You can ground your email strategy in these three guiding principles:

- Know your audience

- Have a plan

- Build trust

KNOW YOUR AUDIENCE

We hope we've convinced you by now, email is a powerful relationship-building tool. To harness its mighty power, you need to think about your audience in every piece of your strategy. Before you decide what to send them, do everything possible to put yourself in their shoes. Better yet, tap into their mindset when they are in the inbox, getting your message. Think about a specific person who will read your email. What will they think when they see your email? What do you want them to know? How do you want them to feel? When you write for a real person, you will more naturally try to meet their needs. Learn more about your audience using insights from the audience research approaches we talked about in chapter 3.

HAVE A PLAN

Successful email programs have one thing in common. They all plan ahead. Complex organizations should try to stay three to six months ahead of email program plans. This amount of lead time gives you enough time to resource your campaigns, from visuals to storytelling, messaging, and other creative needs.

BUILD TRUST

If your end goal is to drive people to take action, you need a trusting relationship. You already know how to build trust; remember that Trust Triangle? You must be authentic, empathetic, and logical.

As you build trust with your audience, design the email experience in a way that builds good email habits in your reader. You want your reader to be in the habit of seeing your email in the inbox, opening it, and clicking on something in that email every time.

PRESENTING YOUR STRATEGY

It's good to start a strategy document with a purpose. For most email programs, their purpose is to connect people with an organization, company, or other people. The purpose of those connections is usually to drive people to take some kind of action.

Stating a purpose for your email program sets the stage for the work and aligns your strategy with larger organizational goals.

Your strategy should outline who is in the email audience, the size of the audience, and any important segments. Use your strategy document to set standards related to meeting reader needs and operating procedures to ensure quality email content is baked into your strategy.

Use your strategy documentation to highlight key collaborators, technology requirements, and your email program roadmap. Be aspirational in your future plans and specific about the things you need to get there.

GETTING DOWN TO TACTICS

We say "getting down" because strategic planning is a very top-down process. You need to set business goals, align them with audience needs, and decide on a strategy that works for both.

It can take years of experience to understand when to discuss strategy and when to talk tactics. Tactics should be informed by your strategy. Strategy comes first.

Tactics are what we do to achieve shorter-term objectives that support a long-term strategy. They are practical, concrete steps. Tactics relate to your strategy in a way that makes the work more focused, detailed, and time-bound. They involve specific activities, tools, techniques, and workflow processes to execute the email program successfully. They are flexible and can be adjusted based on changing circumstances or feedback.

Your email strategy answers "What are we sending" and "Why are we sending it?"

Your tactics will answer "How are we sending it?"

SOME TACTICS ARE A GIVEN

Email programs should account for tactics that are reliable standards (or "best practices") and tactics that are circumstantial and need to be decided on a case-by-case basis.

Reliable Tactics—"Email Standards"

- Use a recognizable "from" name
- Subject lines should be nine words or less
- Use preheader copy (the preview text that appears in the inbox) when it is available
- Use a conversational voice
- You'll see a lot more of these in chapter 6

Circumstantial Tactics—Decided on a Case-by-Case Basis

- Use a person's first name

You can use a person's first name in an email if you would address them by their first name in person. In these cases, the use of first names will increase engagement rates.

- Additional opt-out language

Add empathetic messaging in your email with a clear path to opt out of communication. Use the space to explain why the reader is receiving your email. This tactic decreases opt-outs.

APPLYING GUIDING PRINCIPLES

There's no one way to build an email strategy. Your approach will vary based on your audience, their needs, your organization, its needs, and everyone's goals. The rest of this chapter offers guidance on applying strategic planning principles to email marketing funnels, newsletters, interpersonal emails, and call-to-action campaigns.

MARKETING FUNNELS

A funnel starts wide, with a fixed audience, and then narrows over time, just like the shape of an actual funnel. At each step of the funnel, people will move on or drop out.

Example 1: 5K Fundraiser

Let's imagine you've been hired by a local nonprofit to develop their email program for a 5K road race, the organization's largest annual fundraiser. Your one-line strategy might be: *Inspire runners to register and fundraise for a local 5K event.* How would you apply the guiding principles to this email program?

Step 1) Get to know the audience. In this example, the audience is past participants, local community members, and farther-reaching running enthusiasts.

To understand this audience quickly, you'll want to gather data. You can learn about past participation and where they came from. Data review won't, however, tell you why they participated or what motivates them to fundraise.

You might decide to host a focus group, conduct interviews, or survey past participants and community members to learn more about their motivations and experiences.

Step 2) Create a marketing plan. Plot out all the emails while noting the audience and send dates.

Funnels require a plan that follows someone through multiple steps. In this case, we need an email plan to (1) recruit runners, (2) activate them as fundraisers, (3) support their fundraising efforts, and (4) steward their running and fundraising activities. And we know we need to move all people though this funnel by race day. All this audience-centric planning will inform which emails we need to send.

The recruitment email suite would include a save-the-date message, registration launch messaging, deadline reminders, and as many other reminders to register as the audience can take. Use your unsubscribe rate as a gauge for email tolerance.

The activate suite would help onboard runners as fundraisers, connect them to the cause, and explain why fundraising is important for the organization and the community they support.

Other fundraising support content can be shared with those engaged with fundraising. The more engaged participants are, the higher their tolerance for additional email. Be careful not to overwhelm readers with information they haven't demonstrated interest in.

Finally, you'll need a plan for general communication about the race and a plan for thanking and acknowledging all the actions they took. This communication goes to everyone who made it through the funnel.

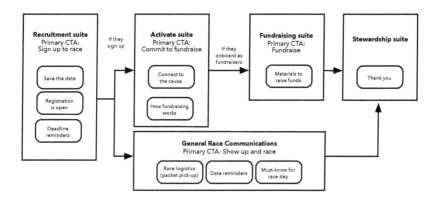

Step 3) Build trust. Review email content for authenticity, empathy, and logic.

If you're designing an email funnel, you're taking someone on a journey. You already know you have some milestones you want the reader to meet and actions you want them to take.

Start with empathy mapping the email funnel. Anticipate how someone might feel each time they receive your email and meet them with that emotion.

For the group of runners that you need to convince to fundraise, consider their time. Let them know it takes only a few minutes to set up an online fundraiser (if that's true). Provide them with sample text messages to send to friends. Make their personal fundraising link easy to copy and share.

As you draft your messages, check your tone for authenticity. Cut unnecessary words and be clear with calls-to-action.

Example 2: Student Enrollment

In this example, you are the enrollment marketer for a college and you're trying to get high school students interested in attending your school, applying, and ultimately enrolling. How would you apply the guiding principles to this scenario?

Step 1) Get to know the audience. How do students and families evaluate colleges and ultimately decide where to go?

Typically, they go through four stages: awareness (do they know you exist?), consideration (do you meet the minimum requirements to be put on a short list, like affordability and program of interest?), evaluation (after they've been admitted, do they feel like they could belong there and reach their goals?), and commitment (after depositing or accepting, what do they need to do to make attending a reality?).

Step 2) Create a marketing plan. For each stage of this enrollment funnel, determine the action required to move to the next stage.

To move from awareness to consideration, they need to subscribe and request information.

To move from consideration to evaluation, we want them to visit and apply.

To move from evaluation to commitment, we want them to pay their enrollment deposit.

In your marketing plan, include the information the reader needs to be ready to take the action that moves them to the next stage. List all the questions they might have that are keeping them from taking action and send them the answers. The trick here is to include just enough for them to take the action. If you don't send enough information, they might not act at all. But if you send too much information (perhaps things that will become relevant later), they might get overwhelmed and not act.

Consider how many emails you want to send. We recommend more frequent emails with less content, one topic at a time. Plan the topics to coincide with the stage your reader is in. For traditional undergraduate prospective students in our example, stages coincide nicely with academic calendar milestones. For more flexible programs you can align your emails with the actions your reader takes.

Step 3) Build trust. In this example, segmentation is very important. You want to get as specific and relevant as possible. If there are groups of students who need different information, like transfer students or international students, only send them the information they need. If your emails contain information that's not relevant to your reader, it will take them more time to unpack the information. It's a poor experience and you will erode trust quickly.

To go above and beyond, apply empathy to this funnel. Consider the emotions they are feeling and adapt your tone. Think creatively with your content: What else may be happening in their lives outside the enrollment process? Maybe these students need study tips, maybe their parents need entertainment while sitting at sports meets, maybe little siblings need pages to color. Don't miss your opportunity to delight.

NEWSLETTERS

Email newsletters get a bad rep. The purpose of a newsletter is to maintain consistent communication with your audience. We believe a thoughtful newsletter strategy is one of the most powerful relationship-building tools there is.

Step 1) Get to know the audience. Newsletter audiences are your most loyal followers. Readers opt-in to regular updates on top of the other transactional emails they might receive from your organization.

Remember our tip: Be thoughtful about what you want to know about your subscribers and ask those questions when they sign up.

Step 2) Create a marketing plan. Newsletters should be sent on a frequent and consistent basis. We recommend at least once a month. And we've seen successful email programs that send letters morning and night. For most organizations, the sweet spot is somewhere between every two weeks and three times a week.

Timing is important. Send your newsletter early in the morning (like getting your morning paper), right before lunchtime, or in the evening when people like to consume news and open their mail.

Step 3) Build trust. Readers should be able to rely on your consistent message cadence and consistent quality in each email you send.

Quality newsletters meet readers' needs. If you don't have anything quality to send, it's OK to skip a newsletter. More importantly, give yourself the flexibility in your newsletter to maintain a high-quality standard. For example, if you hold yourself to completing a rigid newsletter template that requires you to share four news stories and three event links, you risk sharing sub-par content just to meet a self-imposed rule.

Your readers will trust you more if you send them quality content. They will also trust you more when they can rely on you to deliver your newsletter on a predictable schedule. A solid monthly frequency will help your overall sender reputation. More frequent newsletters are often welcome by engaged readers. Use your unsubscribe rate as the metric for understanding when the frequency has become overwhelming for subscribers.

INTERPERSONAL COMMUNICATION

There is a right way to send an email to your colleague. The guiding principles are the same. Think about who you are sending to. Are they busy? How much time do they have to read your note? What do you need to share with them? What do you want them to do?

Step 1) Get to know the audience. Does this person want an email from you? Or do they prefer you pick up the phone, send a text or chat, or walk over to see them? The best way to determine an individual's communication preferences is to ask. Presuming they want to receive your email, interpersonal emails should follow the same norms as interpersonal conversations.

Address the person the same way you would if they were standing in front of you. Consider their time in email time, which is seconds of attention the first time they read your message through.

Step 2) Create a plan. One-to-one messages rarely require a marketing plan. But it is smart to plan for follow-up messages.

Step 3) Build trust. The same rules apply. Be real, be helpful, be clear.

CALL-TO-ACTION EMAILS

The best call-to-action emails are concise. They get right to the point—whether you're writing to boost sales or get out the vote. Be careful with call-to-action emails that miss context. If your reader isn't already aware of what you're doing and isn't connected to you, getting them to act will be difficult. Let's walk through the strategy steps one last time.

Step 1) Get to know the audience. The better you understand your audience, the better you will be able to segment and target call-to-action emails. When you narrow down your audience segments to the people most likely to take action, you can expect better email performance and a higher conversion rate. It's worth the extra messaging effort to speak more directly to target segments. You'll see results in the overall turnout for your campaign.

Step 2) Create a marketing plan. Call-to-action emails should be part of a series of communication that includes awareness-raising and connection-building messages. Consider this fundraising example:

Your local public radio station offers a branded tote bag to each person who makes a gift of $100 or more in the last two weeks of May.

- Email one: explanation of the offer
- Email two: explanation of why the campaign will make a difference
- Email three: direct ask to make a gift
- Email four: reminder to make a gift
- Email five: last chance to make a gift

The messages in emails one and two are important to set the stage and help persuade more people to take action. Emails three through five have the most direct call-to-action messages. The messaging changes as time passes and the urgency to act increases.

Step 3) Build trust. Many call-to-action emails are successful because of engagement campaigns that take place concurrently. A high-performing email newsletter will have a positive effect on call-to-action email conversions.

Use segmentation to put only the best offers in front of each person. When possible, use segmentation based on the reader's own demonstrated interests and prior behaviors.

TIMING AND AUTOMATION

If you have software available to automate sequences of communications, there are situations when it's very beneficial. But it isn't always necessary. Let's look at the difference between triggered and scheduled emails.

TRIGGERED VS. SCHEDULED SENDS

One is not better than the other. What's best depends on what you're trying to accomplish.

Scheduled sends are aligned with the calendar (like timing your newsletter to arrive with your reader's morning coffee). Triggered emails can be set to a planned sequence of messages in pre-established intervals (aka, a drip campaign) or based on your reader's behavior (an action they take). The important thing here is the order. Break down complicated actions into smaller steps and send emails in the order your reader needs to make forward progress.

How do you choose?

A triggered email sequence based on behaviors will create an individualized journey for your readers. This works great for ongoing campaigns, where people can drop in and complete tasks at their own pace. Triggered email campaigns will be more challenging if you have a deadline you're working toward (like a big event). Any marketing campaign with a preset schedule can plug right into a scheduled-send approach.

Mature email operations will have both triggered emails and scheduled emails planned during the same time. Your date-specific emails need to be scheduled separately from other automated emails. In both scenarios, your reader is benefiting from getting your messages at the right time.

The Best Time to Send Emails

Gotcha! There is no best time to send emails. It 100% depends on your audience, the message, and the action your reader needs to take. Here's what you should consider:

Send Date

Dates are only relevant if there is something date-dependent in your email.

Give your reader the time they need to take an action. That's what matters most. This timing varies. For example:

DATE-SPECIFIC EVENT	WHEN TO SEND FIRST EMAIL
Membership expires	4 weeks prior
Online webinar	1-2 weeks prior
In-person visit that requires travel	8-12 weeks prior
Application closes	3-4 weeks prior

These are just estimates. Use them as a starting point. You know your readers best. How much time do they need? Give readers enough time, but not so much they postpone taking action, get distracted, or lose momentum.

Day of the Week
If you search for the best day to send emails, you'll get recommendations from seemingly reputable sources. They're bogus. Because the best day to send emails is the best day for your reader to receive them, and how does a random blog post from 2018 know your reader? It doesn't. Instead, think about your reader's routines. Do they work or go to school during the week? Are their weekends filled with activities? Is what you're asking them to do work-related or leisure-related? On which day might they be more inclined to either of those? We can't give you a magic answer, because it really depends on your reader.

Time of Day
Understanding your reader's typical day can provide insight into when to send your emails. Consider their routines: When do they typically start their day? When are they busiest? When do they have the time to read your email and act upon the information you sent? These insights can help you pinpoint the optimal times for email delivery. We can tell you this: Avoid action emails at times of day when people might be hungry. That's not good for anyone.

Some email service providers will allow you to match your readers' time zones. This is a great option for outreach around the globe! It will require a bit more planning, however: These schedule sends will need to be finalized at least 24 hours in advance to reach everyone at the optimized time of day.

Frequency
Establishing a predictable, regular cadence is important to build trust. Look at your plan. How many emails do you need to send for any given stage? Space them out at equal intervals so they learn to expect (and eagerly await!) emails from you.

Use these tips to get started. Then, monitor your email performance closely. Make incremental changes based on when people open your emails (or don't), when they are clicking, and when they take actions on your website. Adjust the send day or time, or change the frequency to see these small adjustments improve your results. Syncing up with your reader to deliver them the right message at the right time is much more an art than a science.

Key Takeaways

- You need a clear strategy to have a successful email marketing program. The work involves understanding your audience, planning ahead, and building trust with readers through authentic and empathetic messages.

- There are different types of email campaigns, such as marketing funnels, newsletters, interpersonal emails, and call-to-action campaigns. You can apply the same guiding principles to any campaign to define a strategy and start meeting your goals.

- Delivering quality content that meets the readers' needs should be part of your strategy. Be consistent in your email frequency and allow your campaigns to flex to match readers' preferences and engagement levels.

Chapter 5

EMAIL DESIGN AND FORMATTING

How many times have you heard (or said) the phrase "people don't read email"? Well, they're right. Because people in fact do not read email, not in the way you sit down to read a novel, or how our grandparents used to read letters, or how we all imagine ourselves sitting romantically sipping a warm tea with our favorite magazine. That's not how people read emails.

People *skim* emails. To skim is to go over something fast, without comprehending the details. Remember our evidence from chapter 2—41% of emails only get 2–8 seconds of your reader's attention, and another third get even less time!

When a reader gets an email, they make very quick decisions. They decide within seconds if they're going to open the email based on the sender and subject line. And once they open it, they only invest a couple of seconds in figuring out what the email is about and whether it's worth any more of their time.

Here comes the most important lesson in this book. You need to optimize your email layout so your reader sees what you want them to see. In 2 seconds. We're going to show you exactly how to do this, through intentional formatting.

FORMATTING AN EMAIL

Emails are incredibly flexible, which is why you've likely seen hundreds of layouts in your inbox. But there are three basic principles that, when used together, guarantee that your email is skimmable:

1. Headings
2. Styling
3. White space

HEADINGS

One of the most common ways to skim is to hop from heading to heading. Make these work for you by using short headings that describe the content within each section.

If the heading is interesting to your reader, they will want to know more and will read the content in that heading block. If they're not interested, they'll skip the entire section. And that's OK! We can get our messages across if we use the heading real estate wisely.

Headings Are Not Categories

Please don't fall into this trap! Using category names as headings is a big mistake. We see it all the time in templated newsletters. There will be a "News" heading, "Events" heading, and so on. If the reader only skims those words, is your message getting across?

Use the heading space to describe the event, story, or message in each section. Instead of "News," find a few words about the type of news or the top news story in the section; instead of "Events," call out the most interesting or next upcoming one.

STYLING

Styling (some might call it text formatting) uses bold, italics, underlining, or colors to make text look different from the stuff around it. In email, styling can be used very effectively to help your reader get your point fast.

Here are some tips to make styling work for you:

1. Only style the key words your reader must absolutely see in their first skim. Generally, this will only be three to four words and might include an important date or the action you want them to take.

2. Do not style full sentences or paragraphs—this voids the effect and the entire text will be skipped over.

3. Reserve underlining for hyperlinks. This ensures your content remains accessible.

WHITE SPACE

White space is important because your reader's eyes are naturally drawn to whatever is in the center of it. You can use this same principle to call attention to the most important thing in your email: the call-to-action.

If your email has a call-to-action, separate it from the rest of the text by using space before and after. We see this most commonly displayed as a hyperlinked button, but it can also be a plain text link, or a written action like "Reply to this email" or "Stop by tomorrow at 9:00 a.m."

White space serves as a palate cleanser between sections, and when added before and after headings, it makes them easy to skim too.

COMMON READING PATTERNS

Reading pattern is a term used to describe how human eyes read messages on the web. The first and most popular study of online reading patterns was conducted by the Nielsen Norman Group (NNG) in 2006.[11] In this study, they found most people read in an F-pattern.

---

11 Nielsen, Jakob. "F-Shaped Pattern for Reading Web Content (original study)." *Nielsen Norman Group* April 16 (2006). https://www.nngroup.com/articles/f-shaped-pattern-reading -web-content-discovered/.

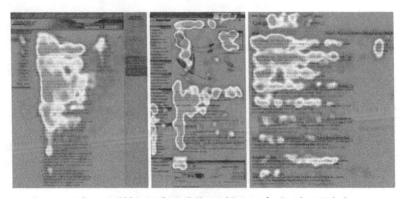

Source: Nielsen, J. (2006, April 16). F-Shaped Pattern for Reading Web Content. *Nielsen Norman Group.* https://www.nngroup.com/articles/ f-shaped-pattern-reading-webcontent-discovered/.

Aptly named, the F-pattern appears when a reader is looking at text on a website. The reader's eyes will follow the shape of a capital F:

- They will read the first horizontal line of text

- Then a second, sometimes shorter, horizontal line of text around the middle

- Then they will skim the first few words down the left-hand side

In countries where reading happens right-to-left, NNG found the F-pattern persists, but flipped.

In 2017, NNG released updates to the study.[12] In the 11 years since the study had come out, websites had evolved, and naturally so did reading patterns. There was an emergence of other ways to read copy, influenced by the evolution in web design. However, they also confirm that the F-pattern is still very prevalent, especially when there are blocks of text to read. This updated study also showed that

---

12   Pernice, Kara. "F-Shaped Pattern of Reading on the Web: Misunderstood, But Still Relevant (Even on Mobile)." *Nielsen Norman Group* November 12 (2017). https://www.nngroup.com/ articles/f-shaped-pattern-reading-web-content/.

(1) visuals like images or videos do not alter reading patterns and (2) the same reading pattern behavior occurs on mobile and smaller screens . . . including emails.

For the purposes of building effective emails, we want to show you two email layouts and demonstrate how headings, styling, white space, and reading patterns work together to optimize skimmability and increase the probability that your readers will see what you want them to see and do.

F-Pattern

The F-pattern is ideal for emails that have a single point or a single call-to-action.

If the eyes will look at the information following an F-pattern, then you want to put all the important details and call-to-action in the areas where the reader's eyes would naturally go.

1. Name the action or important point in the first sentence.

2. Include a button or link where the second horizontal line would be. Surround it with white space.

3. Direct the eyes to other important information by using styling. This is great for dates and reinforcing the CTA.

4. Include more information as a bulleted list after your button. Remember, the reader's eyes are only scanning the left-hand side, so they will only see the first few words of your sentences. Make sure your bullet points lead with the information they *must* see first.

5. If the email has to be longer than what would fit in a typical F shape, add white space and headings to break up the extra content.

F-Pattern Template

Use this template as a summary of how to use the F-pattern to your advantage. Your reader will only read the text in black.

Dear Person,

It's time for you to do this action. No one reads this. No one reads this. You need to do **action** by **date**.

Do the action

Here are some details. No one reads this.

- **Read first word,** but read nothing else.

- **Also this one,** but read nothing else.

- **Less likely this one,** but read nothing else.

- Force them to **read by bolding.**

Last chance to get their attention.

Say goodbye with your niceties,

Sign your name.

Hold Up on the Niceties

Think about almost every email you've ever written or received. How does it start?

> Dear friend,
> I hope this email finds you well.

We, too, hope your friend is well . . . but with this opening line the email might not find them at all. Remember, your first line is crucial because it's the first (and maybe only) thing your reader will see.

This might be the hardest habit to break: Stop leading your emails with niceties. Start every single sentence and bullet point with the action or point you are trying to communicate. If you must include a nicety, flip the sentence order, and add it after the important stuff.

 If you have time, would you please fill out this form?
Fill out this form, if you have time, please.

This word order applies to messages throughout the entire email as well. Instead of starting your email with a nicety, end it with one! Instead of "Best Regards" or "Sincerely," your sign-off is a fantastic spot to wish people nice weather or send greetings to a mutual friend. As a bonus, having a unique sign-off adds personality to your email in a way that might be subtly delightful.

LAYER-CAKE PATTERN

Layer-cake pattern is most common in emails that contain information in sections divided by headings, like newsletters.

Readers skim from heading to heading. Fans of *The Great British Bake Off* TV show can imagine this as a beautiful cake with multiple repeating layers of sponge and jelly. Readers jump from jelly to jelly, eating sponge only if they liked that layer's jelly.

Keeping in mind where the eyes will go in this pattern, here are the important considerations:

1. Make your headings descriptive of the content in the section.

2. Bring attention to content within a section by using styling, like adding hyperlinks or bolding.

3. Add white space before and after headings.

Layer-Cake Template

Dear Person,

No one reads this, unless you make it cute.

Event on date

They won't read this unless they are interested in the heading.
Sign up for event.

Activity for you

Info about this. They won't read this unless they are interested
in the heading. **Prepare for the activity.**

News about person

Info about this. They won't read this unless they are interested
in the heading. **Read person's bio.**

One more thing

Info about this. They won't read this unless they are interested
in the heading, unless you **bold it like this.**

Use this sign off as a brief moment of delight (or not at all).

OTHER PATTERNS

The Nielsen Norman Group has identified many other reading patterns over the past decade, like the spotted pattern, marking pattern, bypassing pattern, commitment pattern—these new reading patterns emerge as designs change.[13] In our experience, because of how emails

---

13   Moran, Kate. "How People Read Online: New and Old Findings." *Nielsen Norman Group* April 5
     (2020). https://www.nngroup.com/articles/how-people-read-online/.

tend to look, F-pattern and layer-cake continue to be the most popular and effective.

The powerful thing about understanding the foundations of formatting an email is now you can make any reading pattern you want using your very own combination of headings, styling, and white space. The eyes will go to the things you choose to highlight with these basic principles.

CHECK YOUR FORMATTING WITH THE 2-SECOND TEST

One way to check if you're formatting effectively is to use the **2-second test**.

Ask a colleague or friend to look at your email for *only 2 seconds*. (You can do this yourself, but only if you promise to be honest.)

What do they remember? It should be what you want them to know, the action you want them to take, and any additional important information to take that action, like date, deadline, location, etc.

If those things do not immediately jump out, rework your headings, styling, and white space so that they do. Use the templates we provide as your cheat sheet—we promise they work.

VISUALS AND MULTIMEDIA

A picture is worth a thousand words . . . or is it?

If you've decided to use visuals in your email, there are several things you need to consider. Not every person receiving your email will be able to see images or access files, for instance, if they are using a screen reader, their email client blocks your content, or they have a slow connection.

Most importantly, **your email copy should be able to stand on its own**.

You cannot rely on visuals and multimedia to share important information or make your call-to-action—these details must always be written in the email copy. Be mindful of the size of any multimedia in your email, because excessive file sizes will prevent your email from being delivered.

BANNERS

Banners are good for keeping brand consistency across messages. Most often, they include a logo or slogan, and might also include a photo that conveys the personality of your brand.

Banners can be effective at adding consistency to series of emails or reinforcing your brand. If you are using banners and they are not serving any specific purpose, consider removing them. At best, they are getting ignored, and at worst, they might be a distraction keeping readers' attention off your copy.

Banner Sizes and Position

The most common position for a banner is right at the top of an email. When placed at the top, banners tend to be shorter than they are wide, a proportion that has become popular because it allows some text to show above the fold.

There is no rule that says banners should go at the top. Especially if you are using photo banners, try different placements in your email. At minimum, changing the position of the banner will keep your emails more interesting.

As for size, there is also no rule that dictates a "correct" size. Optimize your images to the smallest file size where they still display beautifully. Organizations aware of their carbon footprint might choose to not include images at all. Each time an image loads it uses energy. So be mindful and think about the function of the email banner. If your banner is supporting your message by illustrating a space, or setting the mood or vibe of your email, it could take up more space. Make decisions based on what will help and not distract readers from skimming your copy.

Bottom line: You don't need a banner, it doesn't need to be at the top, and it doesn't need to be a certain size. You have the power to decide if you use one, where you place it, and how big it is based on what you want your banner to do.

IN-LINE IMAGES

Images are an alternative to white space. If used correctly, they can break up sections to make it easier for your reader to skim.

Images can help add context. When used in conjunction with a headline—especially as newsletter section dividers—they can help your reader absorb information faster.

However, if the images included have no relation to the copy, or if there are too many images, they can have an opposite effect. They will then create confusion and keep the reader from actually taking in your copy.

ICONS

Icons are illustrated images that can often convey a message very clearly.

Use icons surrounded by white space. Find images that have conventional interpretations that do not arouse confusion, and once again, only use them when they create clarity and serve a specific purpose. For example, when you see social media icons in an email footer, you know these are quick links to the sender's social accounts.

If you use icons, stay consistent with colors and sizes and across emails. Providers like Font Awesome and Noun Project are great places to find these useful visuals.

VIDEO

As of this book's publish date, there is still no smooth way to include video in email.

The standard practice (until someone creates a better solution for us) is to upload the video to a hosting site (like YouTube, Vimeo, or your own website) and place a link to the video in your email. If there is a message in the video you want your reader to know, make sure that is also communicated through your email copy.

When you link to a video in your email, make sure your link text is descriptive, like "Watch this video for DIY instructions." You can also include an image thumbnail or animation of the video and make it clickable. If you do, make sure you're also linking it via text, since not all readers will see your image.

ANIMATION

Animated images, like GIFs, can add a lot of fun to your emails. These are still slightly unexpected, and thus capture attention.

Animation can be used following the same principles as images: to add context or showcase your brand. One of our favorite examples of animated images is Bart Caylor's welcome email to his new subscribers. He sends a quick animation of him waving hello and your first name. Through the personalization and animation, he forms an instant connection. This is one of his core brand values, and this use of animation portrays that perfectly.

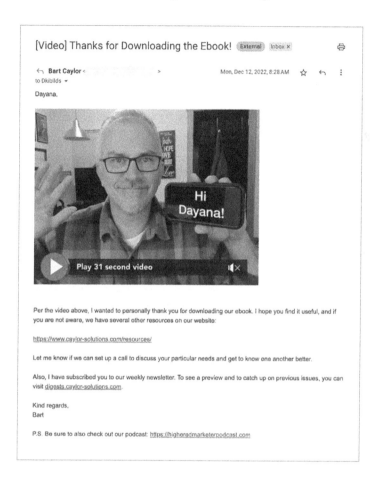

ATTACHING FILES

Large files can prevent emails from being delivered.

If you are sending emails to a large list, the best practice is to upload the attachment to a cloud service and send a link to download instead of the file itself. If you are just sending emails to your internal colleagues, attachments are fine as long as they are under your provider's file size limits.

In either case, the copy within your email must stand on its own. Don't send the content of an email just in a PDF (K–12, we're looking at you 👀).

A Cautionary PDF Tale from One of Your Authors

Dayana: Once upon a time in a past job at a university, I was at a planning retreat with the entire university's leadership team. President, vice presidents, provosts, and the like. During one of the breaks, I was at the snack table trying to calculate the healthiest cantaloupe-to-pastry ratio when I noticed our university's president sitting at a chair in the hallway, scrolling, pinching, zooming, and staring intently at his smartphone. "Work doesn't stop, huh?" I said, clearly distracting him. His response? "I have so many emails, and I'm trying to read them, but the information is in PDFs, and the text is so small I just can't see."

His life would have been easier, and the sender waiting for a response would have gotten an answer faster, if the information had just been written in the email.

Your reader should not need to read an attachment to know what you want to tell them. Attachments are not skimmable, and remember, your primary goal is to get your readers to get the gist of what you're sending within a 2-second skim. If you do that well, your email (and the PDF) will get the attention you want it to get.

HTML VS. PLAIN TEXT

HTML allows you to design visually appealing emails with different fonts, colors, images, and spacing to portray your brand and enhance your content. Plain text emails are exactly that: plain text.

Most email clients give readers the option to choose if they want to receive HTML or plain text emails. This is why it's important to write the key points in your email copy, because not every reader will see your HTML design.

Due to the rise in email as a promotional channel, readers have been accustomed to seeing designed emails as promotional (and sadly, irrelevant), and unless it's something your reader is expecting, they might be more likely to ignore it.

Because of this behavior change, we're seeing a rise in popularity of the plain text email, especially when what you need to communicate is important, urgent, and directly to the point.

One is not better than the other. It's important to consider the context in which you're sending the email and the context in which it is going to be received and read; then you can choose whether it should be fully designed with beautiful images or left in good old plain text.

This doesn't mean that that designed emails can't be straight to the point, but it does mean that fully designed emails are not always a must—even for marketing purposes.

EMAILS ACROSS DEVICES

If you are a person who works regularly with email (if you aren't you must be one of our family or friends, hi! 👋), you probably sit down in front of a big, well-lit computer screen to craft the emails you want to send.

When you're building the email, you spend the time to get it just right. All the images are aligned. There are no weird line breaks. It's perfect.

But, that's not how everyone will see it. In the past, we would make an event of reading our emails. We would sit in front of our computer, open our inbox, and really spend some time with it, on our big computer screen. Nowadays, folks are reading emails on the go, on many different devices like their tablets, smartphones, and even wearable tech.

Your email is going to look very different on each of these screens.

When you write an email, especially if you're using HTML, you need to use code that will display properly on any screen size and email client. There are a few tools you can use to test your code. Mailchimp has a built-in function to render the email in different sizes. Litmus and Email on Acid also have email testing tools so you can see how your email will render in different email clients like Outlook, Gmail, or Apple and on different screen sizes, too.

The good news is the same basics work no matter what screen size will display your email. Use meaningful headings, styling, and white space, and take advantage of common reading patterns (these apply to small screens too!).

ACCESSIBILITY

This book will only scratch the surface of everything you need to know about accessibility. Right off the bat we recommend these two musts: Accessible Social at accessible-social.com and for our friends in education, the Higher Education Web Professionals Association's accessibility community group at events.highedweb.org/accessibility.

This section includes a summary of the most common accessibility considerations we use in our emails.

ALT TEXT

Every single image you include in an email needs to have alt text. Alt text describes what can be seen in an image so that readers who cannot see it are able to understand the context.

When writing alt text, describe what you see in the image in detail. Is there a person in the image? What are they wearing? What's behind them? What are they holding? Is it an image of a landscape or object? What colors do you see? What shapes do you see?

If you're using an image in an email, it's there to add context. Your alt text should be descriptive so that context comes across. (Sidenote: Writing alt text for an image is a good test to assess if the image adds value to your email or not. If you find your description unrelated to the email, maybe you need to take out the image. Just sayin'.)

SCREEN READERS

Screen readers read the copy in your email out loud, as well as descriptor information for every other element you include. This is why including alt text in your images and buttons is important. But there are a few other elements to consider too.

Headings

Users of screen readers navigate through your email with their keyboards. They can move from heading to heading hitting a key ("H" if they're using the popular screen reader NVDA, for example). If you don't have headings properly set up (using H1 in your code), your sea of text becomes an unfilterable ocean of audio.

Front-Load Your Sentences

This is a tip we gave you for skimmability, and it makes your email more accessible too. Put the most important information in your sentence at the beginning. If the reader wants to skip a sentence and go to the next, they should get the key message up front.

Emojis

We love emojis in email. Every emoji has a universal description you cannot change. Screen readers will read that description as if it was copy in your text. Make sure you know what that description is. You can reference Emojipedia to find it.

Because the emoji description might not match your message as closely as its visual representation, it's a good idea to put it at the end of your sentence. That way it doesn't get in the way of your reader getting the message.

Descriptive Links

Screen readers have an option to skip from link to link. Imagine the experience if all your links are "learn more" or "click here." The person would have no context about what the links are. Your link should clearly state what will happen or what the reader will get when it is clicked.

ACCESS

With access we mean literal access to email. Not every single recipient of your emails will have a steady internet connection or their own device. Not all of them will have unlimited data to download videos and images.

Carefully think about anything extra you are adding to your emails and how that might not be accessible to all your readers. Readers without unlimited data will skip your videos. Readers in rural areas without great connectivity may not be able to see your images or files. Readers who share devices or only have access to a mobile phone for internet access may not have a big screen to read long form content or open attachments.

Keep your formatting simple and true to the principles we introduced in this chapter. Your email needs to be skimmable, and you can make it so with smart headings, styling, and white space.

To quote Sarah Winters, author of *Content Design* and a content design role model for all of us, "Accessibility is usability." Putting these accessibility musts into practice makes your email better for *everyone*, and in fact, you'll see these tips repeated and expanded in the next chapter on how to write emails people will read.

Key Takeaways

- Humans read (skim) emails in predictable patterns that you can use to your advantage with headings, styling, and white space.

- The two most effective layouts for emails are the F-pattern (for single action) and layer-cake (for newsletters), and when used well, they will ensure your reader gets your message. Try the 2-second test to make sure you've optimized your email for all readers.

- Visuals and multimedia can add value but are not a must. Your email copy must be able to stand on its own.

- Accessibility is important. Use headings, add alt text to images, use descriptive link text, consider how emojis might be interpreted, and be aware of mobile/internet connection limitations. Accessible emails are better for everyone.

Chapter 6

WRITING EMAILS
PEOPLE WILL READ

The reason we don't start with this chapter is that even the best writing in the world will not get your email read. You need to understand your readers' mindset and have an email strategy. You could write the best email in the world—but if you're sending it to the wrong people at the wrong time, they won't read it. You cannot get your reader to pay attention to you with great writing alone.

However, because you're diligent and you're reading this book, we know you're going to get the mindset and strategy right. And once you do, the next thing to conquer are the actual words.

Your writing needs to accomplish a few key goals:

1. Get your recipient to open the email.

2. Get them to grasp your main point(s) or request quickly.

3. Clearly explain what they need to know so they take the action you want them to take.

THE INBOX

Dayana: When I was 10 years old in 1995, I got my very first AOL CD. I installed it on my family's computer and created my very first email address: ndck06@aol.com (the n stood for Notorious and it preceded my initials like Notorious B.I.G. It was the '90s, don't judge me)

AOL's "You've Got Mail" alert was the phrase of the era, becoming as famous as Meg Ryan and Tom Hanks. And that's because, email suddenly became something we all had access to. We could all receive email, how exciting! Someone had *something important* to say to *me!*

Fast forward to today. There are countless books on how to manage your inbox and reaching inbox zero. Meanwhile, my husband has over 16,000 unread emails. We are no longer jumping with glee every time "We've Got Mail!" And because our inboxes are so flooded, it's hard for any single email to stand out.

To break through the noise, we have three tools at our disposal:

1. From line

2. Subject line

3. Preheader text (sometimes)

No matter the email client, these are the first words your recipient will see.

Together, they should make it extremely clear: who this email is from and what exactly is in it.

FROM LINE

From lines let your reader know who the email is coming from. In most email clients, the from is the biggest text and the first words they see.

Its role is crucial: The from line signals trust.

When your reader recognizes your name or organization, they understand who the email is coming from and can identify the sender as a trusted source. We're not just talking about scanning for phishing

Desktop view of Gmail inbox, the From is first. The view is similar in
Apple Mail and Outlook, except if a preview pane is present,
the From gets stacked on top of the subject line.

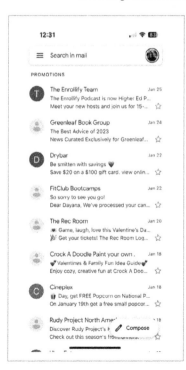

Mobile view of Gmail inbox, the
From is on top, and bigger. Apple
Mail and Outlook are very similar.

and spammers. We're talking about trust that the sender knows the readers they are sending to, and that this email is relevant to their readers. Readers want you to send messages they need when they want to read them.

To draw on the authenticity driver of trust, the from line must display a name your recipient recognizes.

There are many studies out there that say when an email comes from a person rather than an organization, it will perform better. The most recent study we found is from HubSpot[14] in 2023, much to our chagrin. And as much as we want to believe it for simplicity's sake, it's simply not uniformly true. Email open rates increase when an email comes from a person *your reader knows*. But if they don't know the person, they're actually less likely to open it than if the email had come from the name of an organization they recognize.

Take, for example, this Giving Day fundraising campaign at Cornell University. You can see the reader getting emails from many parts of the university. Some emails came from an academic department, some came from non-academic units or groups, and others from the university as a whole. The reader probably does not know who these individuals are, but they definitely recognize the university name, maybe even the department name.

Think about your alma mater. Do you know the name of the current dean of the

Cornell Annual Givi.

Ryan Lombardi

Cornell's Adult Uni.

Cornell University,.

AAP Communications

Sharon Detzer '88

AAP Communications

Engineering AAD Ste.

CUSail

Cornell Annual Givi.

Cornell University .

AAP Communications

AAP Alumni Affairs .

Cornell Giving Day

Office of the Vice .

Cornell Atkinson Ce.

Risa Mish '85, JD '.

Cindy van Es

AAP Alumni Affairs .

14   Cox, Lindsay Kolowich. "23 Email Marketing Tips to Improve Open & Clickthrough Rates [+HubSpot Blog Data]." *HubSpot* March 31 (2023). https://blog.hubspot.com/marketing/make-emails-more-clickable-list.

college you graduated from? You probably don't. Would you be more likely to open an email from a random dean you don't know or from the name of your school? Exactly.

From Lines Can Evolve

If you're in marketing, you probably send emails to people who do not have a prior relationship with you. In this case, the from line should be the words the readers are most likely to recognize, which is probably your brand or organization.

As you continue to develop a relationship with your audience, that from line might evolve and get more specific and might even turn into a person.

Let's use an example from the university search process. When students are in high school, they receive hundreds of emails from schools who want to recruit them. These emails tend to be sent with the name of the college or university as the from line (because that's what the students will recognize).

However, as that relationship evolves and the student becomes more interested in a specific university—even interacts with a specific department or admission counselor—subsequent emails might come from the person they've been interacting with or the department they applied to.

Your from line, once again, matches the name of the person or entity who your recipient has a relationship with at that moment in time—and that can change over time.

This same principle applies to any organization. Start with what they know and get more personal as the relationship develops.

Why Not Both?

To get around the person vs. organization conundrum, some senders try both. You've seen them in your inbox, they look like this: "Johnny from Mentimeter" or "Haley @ Good American."

Our theory is senders started doing this because they read the study that said that people's names increase open rates. They might also think it makes the email look more personable. We think this might be true, if the email is actually coming from this individual. But if their name is just being used and it's yet another mass-market email, readers will see right through this, and the tactic could backfire in the long run.

If combining a person's name and your organization name is something you try, keep in mind the character limitations of the from line space. The max is 20 characters. If you're including a person and organization, write the one they will recognize first. We like this example from a small Canadian business Lezé the Label. Most of their communications come from the company name, but when one of the founders is actually writing to their customers, they add their name to the from line.

	LEZE THE LABEL	Jan 8
	New Year, New Goals 🎯	
	We did incredible things with you last year, and we know... Inbox ☆	

	LEZE THE LABEL	12/30/23
	WHOA! Look at what you did! 🎉	
	We could not have made this impact without you! ... Inbox ☆	

	LEZE THE LABEL	12/26/23
	HAPPY HOLIDAYS! 💜	
	Thank you for being part of our incredible community. ... Inbox ☆	

	Karen at LEZE	12/20/23
	TIME OFF: For the Holidays	
	Hey Dayana, we are taking some time off for the holiday... Inbox ☆	

	LEZE THE LABEL	12/14/23
	Design our FW24 Line!	
	Yes, we are already thinking about what to bring you in ... Inbox ☆	

	K & T at LEZE	11/30/23
	SURPRISE! 🎉	
	We want to give you an exclusive 30% off valid until Dec... Inbox ☆	

	LEZE THE LABEL	11/25/23
	Consider the tea SPILT ☕	
	The best small business sales of the year! ... Inbox ☆	

	Karen at LEZE	11/23/23
	Being Vulnerable Is Hard.	
	Hey Dayana, yes, the whole website is 30-50% off right ... Inbox ☆	

Screenshot of Dayana's inbox showing emails from Lezé the Label and how they use the founders' names sometimes.

SUBJECT LINE

Subject lines get a lot of attention, and for good reason: Together with the from line, they are your only chance to get your reader to open the email.

Because of this pressure, it's easy to overthink subject lines. Email marketers have tried every possible trick to craft engaging subject lines, and some have even ventured into exaggerated or misleading territory. In most countries, it's against the law to intentionally mislead someone with your subject line to get them to view a message. And, if your subject lines get too gimmicky, your email is likely to get flagged as spam.

If you Google "subject lines" today, you'll find dozens of stats and tips on how to make them more effective by using the reader's name, or numbers, or particular word combinations. There is no shortage of tips. But the only tip you need is this: The easiest way to write effective subject lines is to **summarize what's in the email in six to nine words.**

Tell Them the Action

If there is an action to take in the email, don't be afraid to make that your subject line too.

This is especially important for emails that are not promotional. If you are sending emails to colleagues or if your reader must do something important, you can tell them that directly in the subject line.

Some examples:

- "Submit your taxes by April 30"

- "Register your child for summer camp"

- "Complete your October expense reports"

- "Fill out this intake form before your visit"

Avoid Spam ✨Vibes ✨

According to Email Tool Tester, one in seven emails get caught by spam filters.[15] Spam filters have gotten much more sophisticated over time, and don't just look at the words in the subject line anymore—they look at the entire context of your email.

It would be impossible to include an exhaustive list of spam words in this book, because it is ever-growing and ever-changing. And as spam filters get more sophisticated, there is more to keep in mind than specific words. A quick Google search will give you a dozen lists of words and gimmicks to avoid.

If we had to summarize our anti-spam tips all into one idea it would be this: Keep it real. Don't lie, don't exaggerate.

Navigate the Fine Line of Urgency

How do you get someone to do something? You create urgency. The catch here is that false urgency will erode trust and could get you caught in spam.

Only use urgency when there is actually a reason to. For example, there is a due date or expiration date, a countdown to a big event, or spaces are running out.

This example shows the same content but two alternative subject lines. You can see the second subject line clearly states what action is in the email and uses a date to create urgency (without spammy vibes).

The time is here! - The moment you've been waiting for in 20 years has arrived! It's your 20th Reunion. --

Sign up for Reunion by June 3 - All your 2002 friends will be there. --

---

15   Wibowo, Inka and Charlotte Evans. "Email Deliverability Test: A Detailed Look at the Best-Performing Tools." *Email Tool Tester* February 28 (2024). https://www.emailtooltester.com/en/email-deliverability-test/.

Use Personalization (This Doesn't Just Mean a Name)

Personalization isn't just using a first name. It is how we demonstrate to the recipient that we've carefully created this email just for them.

If the email includes information that is specific to your reader, include that in the subject line. Seeing words that are directly relevant to them will establish trust and increase the likelihood of them opening the email.

This example by Il Makiage includes the foundation shade perfectly matched for their reader's skin.

This email from VIA Rail acknowledges the reader is traveling soon.

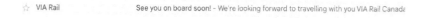

This email from Audible (may or may not have been received by one of this book's authors) is wildly embarrassing, but accurately reflects what the reader is currently listening to. *cough*

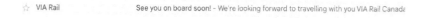

Use Emojis in Moderation and at the End 🖤

One easy way to stand out in a sea of words is with emojis. Emojis can add context and emotion to your subject lines—and they can help you get the attention of your reader in the inbox.

Use emojis only when they add value.

Why? If you use an emoji every single time you send an email, they'll start to lose their effect. Yes, your reader will still see it in their inbox, but readers are very clever and will notice that you are using emojis as bait to get them to open your email. So, to keep your emojis' effectiveness—and your reader's trust in you—save them for when they add value.

To check if an emoji will add value, ask yourself these questions:

- If the reader only looks at the emoji, would it help them know what this email is about?

- Does the emoji add emotion or emphasis to the subject line?

Here are some examples:

- 📅(Calendar) suggests the email has an event in it.

- 🎁(Wrapped Gift) suggests the email has a freebie or gift in it.

- 🖤(Red Heart) evokes the message is loving or caring; bonus branding points if you use a heart in your brand's colors.

- 🎉(Party Popper) suggests the email is celebratory and the tone is exciting.

Even when the emoji adds value, there are important things to consider.

Accessibility
Remember, every emoji has an official name. You can find the names at emojipedia.org. When your reader is using a screen reader, it will read the official name of the emoji as text within your subject line. Be mindful of where you place your emojis so they do not distract or interrupt from your subject line. Never use emojis to replace words. We recommend placing them at the very end and not repeating them.

Different Interpretations
Emojis mean different things to different people, and perhaps more dangerously, many emojis have slang interpretations that are different than what they objectively look like (your homework: Google "Emoji slang guide").

For example, in The Great Millennial vs. Gen Z Debacle of 2022, we learned that a skull means laughing. And if your email includes a recipe with corn, peaches, or eggplants as ingredients, skip the emojis entirely. . .

On a more serious note, emojis can create context if your reader has a similar lived experience to yours or to majority groups. Before you use an emoji, consider how an emoji might be interpreted (or misunderstood) by readers with different identities and backgrounds.

Display Issues

Some email clients won't display emojis at all, or they might show up as Wingdings or empty squares. This is another reason not to rely on emojis to replace words in your subject line, to place them at the very end, and to keep them to three or fewer.

PREHEADER

A preheader (or preview text) is the text that appears next to your subject line, often in a lighter font. Think of your preheader as an extremely effective sidekick. The Robin to your Batman. The Andy to your Miranda.

Use the preheader to provide more information about the subject line, especially if there are more details to support an action, like the time for an event or examples of the giveaway. You can also use it as a literal extension to your subject line, or as a moment of delight. Our favorite trick is this: If the subject line sparks a question, the preheader gives the answer.

When sending mass emails, your email tool will likely have a preheader field you fill out. Always fill it out. If you leave it blank, or if you're sending emails manually without an email tool, the preheader will show the first line of your email.

This is another reason not to waste that first line on niceties (see chapter 5). If you start your email with the point or action you want your reader to grasp, that's what they'll see in the preheader too.

Let's take a look at a few preheaders to make our point.

> Inbox   **HighEdWeb open forum: Nov. 15** - Connect with the board of directors, and share your thoughts abo...

Great, the preheader text tells me what the open forum is about without having to open the email.

> Inbox   **Here's your copy of Litmus' "2021 State of Email"** - Thanks for downloading. It's time to dig in!

A nice stewardship moment following an action taken on the Litmus site.

> Inbox   **Ready for your best year ever with ClickUp?** - Join us in London and kick off the most productive year...

This preheader could work if the subject line was stronger. Is this an event? We can't tell (and we should be able to).

> Inbox   **Does your team need digital strategy skills now?** 📧 - Calling all CMOs, VPs, and Presidents!

Calling out the titles makes this email feel more personal for the reader.

> Inbox   **You're officially subscribed to the Higher Ed Pulse Podcast!** - Get ready for weekly episodes full of in...

Great expectation setting right off the bat.

> Inbox   📧 **My ego hates this ChatGPT trick, but that's why it works** - Read 429 words.   ...

Another great way to set expectations, though it might be better to include an estimated read time.

> **College of Ed in the News** - View this email in your browser   University's Residency Teacher Lic...

This is what happens when you leave the preheader blank. You get the first line of your HTML email "View this email in your browser." Not a great use of real estate!

OVOU Scheduled Maintenance - From 9 PM on Saturday, January 27th, to 1 AM on Sunday, January 28th

Fantastic, maybe TOO fantastic if there are more important details inside, because the reader might decide they have all the info they need and don't open this email.

Inbox Nittany Valley Half-Marathon Volunteers - Hi, I hope this email finds you well! The Nittany Valley Half-Marathon is...

This is what happens when the first line of the email is a throwaway line.

The bottom line with the preheaders is this: Use them! Prioritize clear over clever, but always use them.

AND THE INBOX AWARD GOES TO . . . UBER

The folks who write emails at Uber craft a very effective inbox presence. You can see them employ most of the tips we shared in these emails spanning about three months.

☐ ☆ Uber Eats	Inbox	Beat your hunger for less 🍔 - Play out your savings story.
☐ ☆ Uber Eats	Inbox	Cameron, got room for a discount? 🍴 - Explore more menus serving up offers.
☐ ☆ Uber Eats	Inbox	Stocking up your kitchen is even easier now 🛒 - Check out nearby stores and browse what's new.
☐ ☆ Uber One	Inbox	$0 Delivery Fee 4 months on us - as an Uber One member.
☐ ☆ Uber Eats	Inbox	Get these deals and get in the game - Game Day Deals are here!
☐ ☆ Uber Eats	Inbox	Hungry for a deal, Cameron? - We've got you covered.
☐ ☆ Uber Eats	Inbox	Planning meals, Cameron? Get ingredients in a tap and make the week easier. - Check out nearby stores and browse what's new.
☐ ☆ Uber Eats	Inbox	FREE wings from Wingstop. Winging = winning. - These savings are a slam dunk.
☐ ☆ Uber Eats	Inbox	Stocking up your kitchen is even easier now 🛒 - Check out nearby stores and browse what's new.
☐ ☆ Uber Eats	Inbox	Juicy savings: up to 50% off - Get this offer while it lasts.
☐ ☆ Uber Eats	Inbox	See inside to grab your savings - Restaurants offers too good to miss.
☐ ☆ Uber Eats	Inbox	Get the best of spring with 40% off $50+ (max $35) 🌸🛒 - Shop peak-season produce from your favorite stores.
☐ ☆ Uber Eats	Inbox	Juicy savings: up to 50% off - Get this offer while it lasts.

- Their From is clear and consistent, and the entity the reader has a relationship with.

- They create urgency by including promotion expiration dates ("this week") and creating FOMO ("Deals you don't want to miss").

- Their preheaders support the subject line by providing more information ("Savings up to 30% off") or adding urgency ("Don't let it get away").

- They use sophisticated personalization related to what they know about their recipient, like they've taken trips to and from an airport recently.

- They use a first name, but not in every email. Sometimes it's at the start of the subject line, and other times at the end.

- They use emojis when it adds helpful context to the subject line, and most of the time they are at the end.

INSIDE THE EMAIL

Our work in the inbox did its job, and our recipient has opened the email. Now what?

To write very effective email copy, we rely on tactics that support relevance and readability strategies.

RELEVANCE

Good emails are relevant. In chapter 2 we shared: Relevance is reaching people at the right time with the right message. You execute on this principle with your actual writing by including only the information your reader needs or wants at this point.

- If you're sending an event invitation, include the relevant event details and nothing else.

- If you're sending a newsletter, include the most relevant stories and nothing else.

- If you're sending an email to a colleague asking them to do something, include what they need to know to successfully complete that action.

- If you're sending instructions, avoid steps that may not apply. Use segmentation and other tools like dynamic content to get as specific as you can.

When recipients begin to trust that every word in your email is relevant to them, they will be more inclined to read your emails moving forward.

READABILITY

The next step is to make the relevant content easy to read. Readability is a measure of how complex your words and sentences are, typically reported at a level of formal education.

Yet, you don't need to know your reader's level of education. For general audiences reading content on the web, it's recommended to aim for an 8th-grade reading level.

Nielsen Norman Group found in 2005 that writing at this reading level increases the speed with which your reader understands information and takes action.[16] It also helps keep them engaged without abandoning the task. And these findings were the same for both low-literacy and high-literacy readers!

Doing this is both easier and harder than it sounds. You can get very good at it by following these five tips.

---

16   Nielsen, Jakob. "Lower-Literacy Users: Writing for a Broad Consumer Audience." *Nielsen Norman Group* March 13 (2005). https://www.nngroup.com/articles/writing-for-lower-literacy-users/.

Writing Tip 1: Use Plain-Spoken Words

Write as if your audience has no prior knowledge of your topic. Avoid jargon and acronyms, and use simpler synonyms for complicated words.

Writing Tip 2: Use Active Voice

In active voice, the subject of your sentence performs the action. When you use active voice, you're not dancing around the point the way passive voice does. Don't be afraid to say what you need to say; this is what email is for.

Writing Tip 3: Use a Single-Person POV

Email is very personal. You might be sending it to many people, but every reader is distinct. Treat them that way and consider their point of view. When you write to a single person you'll use "you" instead of more general groups or nouns or phrases.

Writing Tip 4: Use Short Sentences

Avoid compound sentences with many clauses or conditionals. An easy way to make sentences shorter is to remove leading phrases and keep adjectives to a minimum. These are some commonly overused leading phrases and adjectives:

- In order to . . .
- First and foremost . . .
- I'm writing to inform you that . . .
- I was wondering if . . .
- I was hoping you . . .
- Due to the fact that . . .

- There are so many of these, a simple Google search will give you extensive lists of phrases to avoid.

Writing Tip 5: Front-Load Information

The beginning of your sentence should carry the point. (We're saying this louder now for the folks in the back!) If your reader reads only the first few words, they should know what you want them to know. In most cases, you can simply invert the order of your words.

BAD	GOOD
In order to keep your membership active, you must renew by the deadline.	Renew your membership by the deadline to keep it active.
If you have time, would you please take a look at the attached document?	Take a look at the attached, please, when you find the time.
I thought you might be interested in this article about pancakes.	Here's an article about pancakes you might find interesting.

IF YOU FEEL STUCK, STOP WRITING

Until you get used to writing at an 8th-grade reading level, your first email drafts may still be dense and difficult to read.

Try this: Imagine a single person in your audience sitting across from you at your desk or with you in a coffee shop. Say aloud what you want to tell them. Then write down the exact words you just said. This exercise will get you away from the written word and into spoken language, which tends to be more consumable on average. If you use this trick for your first draft, it will be much closer to an 8th-grade reading level. We expect you will still need to edit it to remove niceties and filler words, though.

CHECK YOURSELF WITH ONLINE TOOLS

Once you've written a draft, there are tools that can help you measure your message's readability.

Our favorite is Hemingway Editor at hemingwayapp.com. It's free! Paste your text on the website and it will tell you the overall reading level and highlight the most complicated sentences for you to fix.

Another useful tool is Grammarly, and if you have Premium, it will rewrite complicated sentences for you.

EMAILS WRITTEN BY GENERATIVE AI

We've experimented with GPTs to write emails and there are a few pros and cons. In the time this book goes from being written to being published, we're sure AI will continue to progress, so we're hesitant to put anything down too firmly. But as of the end of 2023, these are the pros and cons we've found with using generative AI to write your emails:

PROS	CONS
• It's very good at turning complicated text into simple text.	• The copy is sometimes verbose and exaggerated, even when you ask it not to be.
• It can generate very easy-to-read content.	• If you simply ask for an email, it will generate copy exactly like we're telling you not to: with niceties at the beginning and unnecessary filler.

We've always been early adopters, especially for digital tools, so we are supporters of AI. But on its own the emails don't quite cut it (yet, we're sure). You can get really solid starting copy, but you'll still need to finesse it with the tips in chapters 5 and 6 of this book—especially when it comes to formatting text, front-loading actions, and design layouts.

ANOTHER IMPORTANT NOTE ON ACCESS

These readability tips help your average reader understand what you want them to do, fast. But there is also an additional dimension that makes relevance and readability extremely important: creating access.

Not all your users will have achieved the same level of formal education. Not all will have peers or family members who can help them read and interpret information. Not all of them will speak your language as a first language. Not all of them will process information the same way or at the same speed.

Writing relevant and readable content is an act of breaking down barriers, and that's something we can all take ownership of.

LINKS

All that work we've done with our subject lines and copy lead to one thing: getting our recipient to do what we want them to do.

Most of the time (though not all of the time) that action will involve clicking on a link or a button.

Text Links vs. Buttons

Campaign Monitor did a test in 2019 and found that their readers were 28% more likely to click on a button than just a text link.[17] While this might make you think that buttons have magical powers, they don't necessarily.

The magic is in the formatting. Buttons are typically a different color or font and surrounded by white space. This makes them different from everything else around them and thus impossible to ignore.

If you are writing an email to a colleague or you send mass emails without design, you might not be able to use a button. Fortunately,

---

17 "Why You Should Use Buttons in Your Email Marketing Campaigns." *Campaign Monitor* May 28 (2019). https://www.campaignmonitor.com/blog/email-marketing/buttons-email -marketing-campaigns/.

the effect is easy to re-create with smart use of white space and font properties. Here is an example of an email we sent promoting our workshops, re-creating the button effect with a text-only link.

Sign up for a workshop on January 19

We're running an online **workshop on January 19 from 1-4 pm ET**. It'll cover the science of email, sending the right message at the right time, and how to write better emails.

Get your tickets

- Early bird at $399 until January 9
- 2-for-1 deal at $319/person (4 of these deals left!)
- Regular at $595
- Full team at $2,500 flat rate

So, instead of talking about text links vs. buttons, let's talk about what really matters: primary vs. secondary actions and what the linked text should include.

Primary Action: Your Most Obvious Link

If the purpose of your email is to get the recipient to do a specific thing, that's your primary action. If that action is something your reader can initiate through a link, then it should be the most obvious link in your email.

Some emails might include actions that are not initiated through a link, like reading, showing up for an appointment, or dining at a restaurant.

Make your priority action the most obvious link by making it look different than what's around it—whether it's a proper button or text surrounded by white space.

Secondary Actions: Links within Text

You can think of secondary actions as optional or supplemental. If your reader is engaged, wants more information, or has time to explore, they are welcome to click and enjoy secondary links for additional context. But your secondary links should not distract them from the main call-to-action, so they should be given less visual weight.

Secondary links can be hyperlinked text found within the sentences of your email's body copy. Unlike primary actions, these links aren't surrounded by white space nor are they very different from everything else around them. They still look like hyperlinks but could be skipped in a quick skim.

Primary and Secondary Links in Action

One of our favorite examples of primary and secondary action links is from the HighEdWeb Association. They include a variety of stories and calls-to-action in each newsletter. They use buttons for the actions they want to prioritize and rely on text links for the rest.

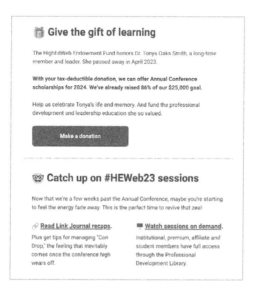

Example of how the HighEdWeb Association uses buttons and links
in their newsletter to indicate priority of actions.

Specific and Descriptive Link Copy

Whether you are using a button or link, your link copy should be specific and describe an action or benefit. If you remember nothing else about links, remember that.

Ask yourself this: If the reader only sees the link, do they know what you want them to do? **The answer should be yes.**

BAD	GOOD
Learn more	Read Ashley's bio
Donate	Donate to save puppies
Click here	Download our photography guide
Register	Sign up for the Open House
Apply	Apply to volunteer
Start survey	Complete the survey for a $10 gift
Subscribe	Connect with 20,000 new best friends

Because hyperlinks are often underlined and in a different color, they are almost always included in your reader's skim. Writing links as the action or benefit helps your reader understand exactly what you want them to do and exactly what will happen when they click—all within seconds of opening your email.

Writing your links this way is also a standard practice for accessibility. Readers using screen readers might choose to just hear a list of links and skip the surrounding text. If your links are not specific, they could miss your message entirely.

A Note on "Learn More"

"Learn more" is one of the most overused call-to-action links today. It's difficult to avoid. Fight the urge to use this phrase. Ask yourself: "Learn more about what?" The answer to that question is your link text.

When You Can't Hyperlink

Sometimes the email client we are using or the recipient we are sending to will not allow us to use hyperlinked text. In this case, include the same specific, descriptive link text you would have linked preceding the actual URL, like this:

- Download photography guide here: URL

- Sign up for Open House here: URL

Including the action or benefit up front helps the reader understand right away what the link is for.

What We're Not Saying: Link Length

By this point in this section, you probably expected us to tell you how long your link text should be, especially in a button. We've been avoiding it because there is no correct answer. But if prescriptive is what you want, prescriptive is what we'll be. So, try this:

- For your buttons, try a maximum of six words. Anything longer than that will just look weird.

- For text links, include the action and benefit, however long that may be, but don't link a full sentence.

PUTTING WORDS AND FORMATTING TOGETHER

When you combine the writing tips in this chapter and the formatting tips from chapter 5, the effect is very powerful. When users skim the way they naturally will (in 2–8 seconds), they'll get as much meaning as they possibly can out of your words.

Here is a fundraising email as it was originally written compared to an email with our writing and formatting techniques applied. Can you tell the difference? Which version helps you get the message in 2 seconds? (We know it's the latter, because these tips work!)

Here is the BEFORE email:

Runners To The Rescue 4 Giving Tuesday Inbox ×

City Marathon   Sat, Nov 28, 2020, 11:47 AM ☆ ↩ ⋮
to me ▾

RUNNERS TO THE RESCUE

CITY MARATHON LOGO   VODKA BRAND LOGO   VODKA BRAND SPONSOR

#RunnersToTheRescue

In the spirit of the **Ruffalo Stampede** and **Dog Days of Summer**, The City Marathon and a vodka brand have joined forces again to support fifteen local animal rescues and shelters.

During this unprecedented time and with many facing joblessness and illness, millions of pets will end up in shelters this year. About half of those pets will be euthanized due to overpopulation. With your help in getting the word out about this opportunity to donate, together we will build awareness to the plight of homeless pets and help to save lives.

Our sponsor is a supporter of dogs and started **Vodka for Dog People** to better the lives of pets and their families far and wide.

In the spirit of **Vodka for Dog People**, our sponsor has offered a **dollar for dollar match up to $15,000** to help us support the fifteen local animal rescues and shelters listed below. Here at the City Marathon we are dedicated to making a difference in the community, so please help us raise the $15,000 to match the vodka brand's generosity. This will ensure each group receives $2,000.

We have until the end of Giving Tuesday (12/1) to collect donations. To date, we have raised $680 from 17 people, which averages $40 per person. If everyone receiving this email donated $5 or $10 we could reach our goal today with time to spare. Please consider joining the effort as well as sharing this message with friends and family.

The following is the email AFTER we applied the techniques described in this book. Can you see how much more effective this is?

From: City Marathon

Subject: Will you help us save the kittens & puppies? 🐶🐱

Hi Day,

Our four-legged friends need our help to live.

Donate to save pets

Due to many fellow humans facing joblessness and illness, millions of pets will end up in shelters this year. About **half of them will be euthanized** due to a lack of resources.

But, if we can raise $30,000 for 15 local shelters, we can save their lives.

A vodka brand has partnered with us to match your donations up to $15,000. This means **every dollar you give will double.**

We've raised $680 so far. Will you donate $10 to save our furry friends' lives?

Key Takeaways

- Decisions to open your email are made in the inbox. Make your from line something the reader will recognize (person or organization), make your subject line describe what's in the email, and use your preheader or preview to help fill in any blanks.

- Use simple language and short sentences when you write emails, aiming for an 8th-grade reading level. Front-load your sentences with the action in the first half.

- Use emojis when they add context or value, and always at the end of your subject lines or headers.

- Prioritize your primary and secondary actions, and make sure your primary actions stand out, either by using a button or surrounding them with white text.

- Clearly articulate the action or benefit in your link text. If your reader only sees your links and reads nothing else, they should know exactly what action is expected and what's in it for them.

Chapter 7

WORKING WITH
STAKEHOLDERS

Within an organization, the marketing team is a service operation. They are the machine that drives communication. They are the creative factory in charge of shipping and receiving messages. Marketers serve their audience and their organization.

In this line of work, there are many reasons you might need to work with stakeholders when planning and writing emails:

- You share an audience.

- Another area has content you need.

- Someone needs to approve email messages.

- You provide oversight of all email sends centrally.

We'll relate to these dynamics (and more situations) through the lens of three key stakeholder collaboration areas: planning, writing, and workflow.

PLANNING WITH STAKEHOLDERS

Planning is the most important part of working with stakeholders. This is how you maintain a sustainable production schedule and keep emails relevant to your audience. If you don't plan communication together, your recipients could get confused, frustrated, and lose trust in your organization.

It's also (on a staff level) how you avoid chaos, drama, and tears. The best way to plan with stakeholders is to…focus on the audience.

1. What does your audience need to know? —▶ Those are your email topics.

2. When do they need to know it? —▶ That's your timing.

3. Who has/owns that information? —▶ That's the partner who is the author or approver.

You can see how from those three questions alone a content calendar starts to form. Depending on the area where you work, you might not know *everything* the audience needs. This is why it's so important that, when there are stakeholders involved, you answer these questions and make a content calendar together.

From there, it's easier to see overlaps and adjust timelines, and for everyone to feel invested in the messages that will be sent out. Not every single email that is sent to your audience will be on this calendar, and that's OK. Any starting point is a good starting point.

The best laid plans are full of opportunities to add more emails and tweak marketing copy. Be sensitive to team members who have invested their time in building the calendar. Email calendars should be built thoughtfully and with lots of good intentions. If an email has to be added, the partners and stakeholders should make a case for it. And if it's a good reason, it's an email that can be documented and planned for the next cycle when you make the calendar again. Over time, your content plan gets more robust and reliable, and you will live in a less reactive and urgent world.

WHAT IF STAKEHOLDERS HAVE DIFFERENT PRIORITIES?

We feel for you. You won't find the answer to that in this book. All we can say over and over is: Focus on the audience. It's not about your partners, and it is not about you.

WHEN IN DOUBT . . . WORKSHOP IT.

Creating a shared content calendar is way easier said than done. We've found it a lot easier to create a shared plan under the guise of a collaborative workshop. We'll give you two models to try.

Creative Brainstorming: Creating Engaging Content with Shared Ownership

Creative brainstorms are great for generating ideas with stakeholders who send regular newsletters to the same audience, year after year.

Our brainstorms go like this:

1. At the start of each quarter, host a brainstorming session with as many stakeholders as you'd like. We like virtual sessions, because more people can participate. The session will focus on generating ideas for the following quarter. We've found this pace gives everyone plenty of time to plan and create.

2. Using an interactive tool like Slido or Mentimeter, give your audience a prompt that makes them think of key dates, activities, and celebrations happening in the next quarter. For example, "Every spring I _____" or "What comes to mind when you think of back to school?" Adjust these prompts based on the quarter that is coming up.

3. Your brainstorm participants will brain dump all the obvious things first, and then more interesting and unique themes will emerge. This part of the exercise generates content ideas at

the same time it gets all your stakeholders in the mindset of
your email readers during that next quarter.

4. After the poll-assisted brainstorm, split up the group into
   smaller groups. Give them a focus: one group charged
   with messaging, one with visuals, one with multimedia or
   download ideas, one with story ideas, whatever you'd like.
   Their job is to use the sparks of inspiration from the first part
   of the brainstorm and further develop the group's ideas.

5. Bring everyone back together and ask each group to share.
   You'll quickly notice the themes that came up more than
   once, from each group. Let them weigh into each other's
   ideas. You'll see dots start to connect, and people start to feel
   excited about the plans that are coming together.

6. End the session, thank everyone. Now it's time for those
   actually in control of resources to assess what is feasible
   and make a plan. Assign a budget. Assign the team. And
   then share this plan back out with all the stakeholders
   who participated.

A few magical things happen with this method:

- Everyone who participates feels ownership and excitement
  for what's to come. As a result, they also understand what
  content will be sent (and what will not).

- When you build your content around a reader mindset like
  this, your newsletters and emails go from being dull accounts
  of what's happening at your organization to relevant and
  interesting content that fits right into the life of the reader.

- These brainstorms are fun. You'll see your stakeholders excited
  to participate in your brainstorms time and time again.

Multiple Perspectives: What We Want to Send vs. What Our Readers Need

Imagine a scenario where multiple stakeholders feel they need to send a ton of information to the same readers in the same time frame. One example from our work is the weeks between when a student submits an acceptance deposit and the first day of class. During this time, schools will want to communicate about tuition fees, housing, orientation, class registration, academic advising, support services— we could go on.

Without coordination, you can imagine the chaos. Here's one way to get ahead of it:

1. Bring together every stakeholder group who wants to send emails to the same readers in the defined period.

2. Give every stakeholder a stack of sticky notes in a unique color. Assign a color to each area (if there are multiple individuals per area, they will share the same color). For example, in the enrollment context, admissions would get blue, residence life would get green, financial aid would get red, and so on.

3. On a wall (virtual or otherwise), draw the time frame you are planning for and split it up into smaller chunks. If you are planning for the summer, split it into months. If you are planning for the year, split it into quarters.

4. Ask your stakeholders to write down every important message they need to send during this time. One message per sticky note. Then, ask them to put up the sticky note on the wall, around when they need to send it.

5. When they're done, ask everyone to step back and look at the board. It will look like a rainbow. Then ask them to step in and look at all the messages one by one. They'll quickly notice duplication, conflicting messages, and different timing.

6. Now, ask them to put themselves in the mind of their readers. As a large group, ask them to design the ideal flow from start to end. What does the reader need to know first, what do they need to know next? Bonus if you can get actual members of your email audience in the room to help you do this. You as the facilitator can write this down in neutral sticky notes and put it up on the wall.

7. Ask your stakeholders to walk up to the wall once again; this time, their task is to rearrange the stickies to match what their audience needs. Group stickies when possible. Discard stickies if they are irrelevant. Finally, for each sticky note or sticky cluster, decide who the sender will be.

8. End the session, thank everyone. Take pictures of the wall and translate it into a digital calendar format and send everyone who participated your shared content calendar.

This method is very effective in bringing stakeholders with competing priorities together. First, it shows them they are not the only ones communicating important things. Second, it makes the negative experience of the reader obvious if they don't coordinate. They'll have ownership and responsibility for the shared content calendar because they created it. There might still be some rogue emails here and there, but the majority of the emails your readers get will be thoughtfully coordinated based on what they need, not on what each stakeholder wants to send.

MANAGING THE CONTENT CALENDAR

Once a calendar is in place, someone must oversee it and make sure it is being followed. Because you're reading this book, we think that person is probably you. But if it isn't, here are a few scenarios to help you consider what your role should be.

WHEN EMAILS HAPPEN CENTRALLY
(AND YOU WORK IN CENTRAL)

If you're lucky to work someplace where all emails are sent from a central office (and you happen to be in that central office), it is easy to keep "control" of the calendar.

What will be important for you is to establish a workflow (tips later in this chapter) that gives you enough lead time to gather content, get emails built, and wrangle any approvals to send.

You are also in charge of upholding the calendar, and if anyone wants to go rogue and send emails outside of the plan, you get to ask some questions and protect your readers.

WHEN EMAILS HAPPEN CENTRALLY
(AND YOU WORK IN ANOTHER UNIT)

This is a hard position to be in! If this is the case, you have to trust that the central unit is also working in the best interest of the readers. While you may not control the email sends, you certainly can have the initiative to start the planning process across the organization. Politically, we know this could be tricky. Put your most earnest, eager-to-help face on, go to central, and propose creating a calendar together across the organization. Suggest one of the workshops we shared. They will either say no because they're too busy (and you can offer to coordinate it all), or no because they don't know how (and you can do it then). If they say no for another reason . . . well [redacted].

WHEN EVERYONE SENDS THEIR OWN EMAILS

Sigh. This is the hardest situation to coordinate. There is no guarantee folks will stick to a plan together. You can still initiate the shared planning process and establish a shared calendar. Lead by example.

To keep it in check, the best way to try is to have regular check-ins with all stakeholders and ask everyone to share email performance stats. Rogue emails might reveal themselves through that sharing process.

We also recommend that all stakeholders receive all emails, so everyone is aware of what's going out and the experience of the readers. We're certainly not above seeding email addresses in your stakeholder's recipient lists to know the real truth.

Remember, when we all work together, we all win trust. When we don't respect our readers, we all lose trust. If everyone understands that, coordinating is easier.

WRITING WITH STAKEHOLDERS

Different relationships require different writing approaches. Here are the most common:

- Someone else is the subject matter expert, you are the writer and approver

- You are the writer, someone else is the approver

- Someone else is the writer, you are the approver

- You are neither the writer nor the approver

Let us give you some strategies for each.

SOMEONE ELSE IS THE SUBJECT MATTER EXPERT, YOU ARE THE WRITER

The easiest of all. Treat this like an interview. Think about what your reader needs to know and ask those questions specifically. If you aren't connecting with the subject matter expert one-on-one, and you're distilling content from other materials, make sure you are adjusting messages in a way that works for email (simple language above all—see chapter 6!).

YOU ARE THE WRITER, SOMEONE ELSE IS THE APPROVER

If your emails have to be approved by a supervisor, a subject matter expert, or anyone else, you can easily fall into difficult feedback loops.

We recommend that you write your first draft in a document stored in the cloud (Google Docs or Box). When you invite your stakeholders to review, give them only comment access. Do not let them rewrite your email. This way, the interaction will feel more like a conversation, and you still have ultimate authorship over the email.

When you request feedback, be very specific about what you want to receive. Do you need them to fact check? Grammar check? Watch for brand tone? Ask specifically. Otherwise, they will give you their opinions on which adjectives they prefer, and that is not valuable feedback.

To avoid approval bottlenecks, give your reviewers a deadline with a consequence, like "send me feedback by April 5, please. If there are no changes by then, I will assume we are good to go!" If they need more time, they will tell you—and then at least you'll know.

SOMEONE ELSE IS THE WRITER, YOU ARE THE APPROVER

Lucky duck. Our advice for you if this is your role is: check that the message aligns with what the reader needs and is written in a way they will understand.

Also, respect your writer's authorship. Unless something is absolutely wrong (incorrect or stylistically off-brand), your word preferences are just that: your preferences. You can let them know if you have an opinion on that, but you can't expect them to change word choices based on your preference.

And, if you find yourself constantly behind and unable to review emails on time, get your operation to run without your review. Can the writer use more training? Can you delegate the approval or at least parts of it? You don't want to be a bottleneck—that's frustrating for everyone involved.

YOU ARE NEITHER THE WRITER
NOR THE APPROVER

This must mean you are managing sends or you are an editor. Editors are my heroes; do your thing. If you are the sender, your eyes on the copy can't hurt. Many a typo has made it past rounds of reviews, and you would be the person to save the day.

CREATING A WORKFLOW FOR STAKEHOLDERS

Here are some steps you need to think about. In the workflow, white bubbles represent a unit or person who builds and sends emails, gray represents the stakeholder. It's up to you and your organization how much time you need for each stage. You might not need all the steps, and not all the steps will be completed by the same person. Building a workflow like this can easily show a stakeholder how much work and time is needed to get their emails sent and how they can hold up the process if they don't do their part.

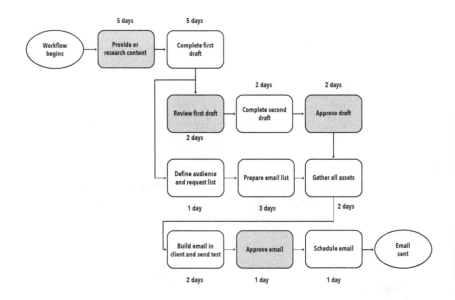

Key Takeaways

- Coordinating and collaborating with stakeholders is crucial to not lose trust with your readers.

- Always prioritize the reader's needs when making decisions about email content and scheduling.

- Build shared content calendars with your stakeholders in advance.

- Setting up a process for writing and approvals will help you reduce last-minute chaos and get your stakeholders in the habit of submitting content early.

Chapter 8

MEASURING

So, you've read the book. You've implemented as many tips as you could. How do you know it's working? There are two things to look at: email performance metrics and the overall performance of your email strategy.

EMAIL PERFORMANCE METRICS

Metrics help you measure the effectiveness of your writing and formatting. To an extent, they also measure the trust your readers have in you as a sender. And if we look at them frequently, they allow us to improve continuously and correct negative trends before they become a problem.

There are many possible metrics to look at. We'll list a few here. It's important that you know exactly how your email client defines and calculates these, since it does vary from one tool to the next.

METRIC	DEFINITION	WHAT IT TELLS YOU
Delivered	Emails that successfully made it to your readers' inboxes. Often reported as a percentage of your total list.	If the email addresses on your list are all correct and active.
Bounced	Emails that did not make it into your readers' inboxes. Most email clients will also give you reasons why the send failed. Hard bounce if it's a permanent error, soft if it's temporary. It's a good idea to clean up your email list using the information from this report.	How many of the email addresses on your list are not correct or inactive.
Opens	Total count of times your email was opened. This will not be 100% accurate due to some email clients that block tracking, emails set to not download images, or viewing emails in the preview pane.	If you sent the email to people that care about its content. If you sent the email at the right time. If your subject line was effective.
Unique Opens	Count of individuals who opened your email, regardless of how many times they opened it.	The same as Opens, but less inflated.
Repeat Opens	Calculated as Opens divided by Unique Opens. It shows you, on average, how many times an individual opened the email.	Repeated engagement with your email, usually because they had to come back to reference or take the action you asked them to.
Unsubscribes	Count of individuals who unsubscribed through the link in that email.	How many individuals decided to stop getting email from you based on this email.
Clicks	How many times any of the URLs in the email were opened. If you link to the same URL twice, this metric does not tell you which link placement was the most popular.	Which links got the most clicks. How effective your link text is. If the recipient had intent to take an action.
Clicks/Open	Also known as click-through rate. Percentage of people who clicked a link after they opened the email.	Percentage of people who are intending to take action after they opened your email.
Clicks/ Delivered	Also known as click-rate. Percentage of people who clicked a link out of everyone who received it.	How many people are taking action out of your whole list. To be honest, we don't love what this one measures. Be careful with how you interpret it, because this metric can be severely impacted by a bad open rate, even when your email copy is perfect.

Click Heat Maps	Heat map view of the most clicked links in your email layout.	Where in your layout do most people click. It's interesting to see how this changes from mobile to desktop.
24-Hour Performance	Opens, clicks, unsubscribes, or other metrics mapped out per hour.	What time your audience engages with your email.
Replies	Number of people who replied directly to your email.	How engaged or confused they are.
Forwards	Number of people who forwarded your email.	How interesting they found the email.
Spam Reports	Number of people who reported your email as spam.	If you are writing in a spammy way. How many people do not trust you.

WHAT MAKES A METRIC GOOD?

If you Google it, you will find countless email metric benchmarks out there. One of the most common ones is Mailchimp's Email Marketing Statistics and Benchmarks by Industry report, which aggregates performance by all their users and shows average metrics by industry.

Here's a look at the average across all industries compared to our industry (Education), the industry with the highest average open rate (Government), and the industry with the highest average click rate (Hobbies).[18]

Average Email Marketing Campaign Stats of Mailchimp Customers by Industry

INDUSTRY	AVERAGE OPEN RATE	AVERAGE CLICK RATE	HARD BOUNCE	SOFT BOUNCE	UNSUBSCRIBE RATE
Average across all industries	21.33%	2.62%	0.40%	0.58%	0.26%
Education & Training	23.42%	2.90%	0.32%	0.51%	0.21%
Government	28.77%	3.99%	0.33%	0.50%	0.13%
Hobbies	27.74%	5.01%	0.18%	0.31%	0.23%

---

18 "Email Marketing Benchmarks and Metrics Businesses Should Track." *Mailchimp.* https://mailchimp.com/resources/email-marketing-benchmarks.

If this table shows the average, any metrics above the average can be called "good." This is true only in the scenario in which you're advocating for yourself and to get more resources at your institution. ("*Look, we're doing better than the industry average—our emails work!*")

In actuality, in order to measure whether your metrics are good, you need to compare against yourself.

ESTABLISHING YOUR OWN BENCHMARKS

Much like Mailchimp's table, create a benchmark table for yourself. Follow these steps:

1. Identify which metrics you care about most.

2. Calculate an average of those metrics over the span of one typical cycle (year, quarters, whatever you'd like).

3. Break down the average by any relevant segment (optional).

4. Break down the average by any relevant categories (e.g., event invitations, transactional, weekly newsletter, etc.).

We break the averages down by segment and by category because emails will perform differently depending on who they're being sent to and what they are about. Get as granular as makes sense to you. One good trick is to focus on the segments you are trying to improve or change (look at your unit's strategic plans).

Once you create this table for the first time, this is your benchmark. During the cycle, you can look at individual emails and see how they're performing against your average. At the end of the cycle, calculate an overall average across all your emails to see if you moved the needle.

IMPROVING EMAIL METRICS

If you are monitoring your metrics continuously, there are certain things you can try to improve from one email to the next. We'll focus on the two most common engagement actions: unique open rate and click-through rate.

BETTER UNIQUE OPEN RATES

When your open rate isn't hitting your own benchmark, there are a few things you can try.

Change the Subject Line

If your email is sent to the right people at the right time, they will want to or need to open it. Make your subject line a six-word summary of the content of the email, and they'll immediately know it's relevant for them.

If your email software allows it, you can use A/B Testing on your subject lines to optimize for the best performing one. Try two variations of the same principle: six words summarizing what is in the email. Remember the important tips: urgency, personalization, maybe an emoji for context or emotion. Once your email software determines which subject line performs best, it will deliver only that one and you will also learn what works best for your readers for all future emails.

Try a Different Send Day or Time

Think about when your readers are getting the email in their inbox. Are they eating? Are they asleep? Are they at school or work? If you send the email when they can't read it, they won't. Check out your 24-hour reports to see when most readers are opening your emails and adjust your day/time to that. If you have the time and resources, try to understand a typical day in the life of your reader and send your email during their down times when they would be most likely to read it.

Segment Your Audience Further

If subject lines are good and timing is good, maybe you're not targeting enough. For the email to get opened, your reader has to trust it is relevant to them. Maybe your list is too broad. Think carefully about your content and the actions in the email—is it relevant to everyone on that list, or only a segment? If the latter, then you need to segment your list further. Segmenting can also help with deliverability, making it more likely your email will end up in the inbox over the junk or promotions folder.

Clean Up Your List

Sometimes low open rates mean your list isn't up to date. Check your deliverability reports. Remove any email addresses that are no longer active. In some cases, you can go a step further. Some email software allows you to see who on your list hasn't opened your emails in a certain time frame. If someone hasn't opened a single email from you in a year, do you still want to be emailing them? It depends. You probably have to if you are legally obligated to report things (like investments, tax-related things, etc.), but it might not make sense if you're sending fun marketing stuff. You can send an email to let them know you're taking a pause from filling their inbox, and they can resubscribe any time.

BETTER CLICK-THROUGH RATES

OK, you're getting past the inbox and your readers are opening your email. But, your clicks are lower than you expect. What can you do?

Nothing

In some cases, maybe nothing. Is a click required for them to get your message? Sometimes the content in the email is enough, and all you need to adjust are your expectations.

Write Clearer Link Text

If your readers read only the link text, do they know what you want them to do? Do they know what will happen when they click? If your links aren't a clear description of the action, they likely will not get clicked on.

Improve Your Formatting/Scannability

If your links are buried in the copy and not easy to pick out in a quick scan, they might get missed entirely. Review chapter 5 and adjust your layout to where the eyes will naturally go.

Use a Button

Using a button increases clicks. If you can't use a button, mimic the button effect by surrounding your link with white space. But don't use too many buttons. Prioritize your top actions.

Try Different Send Times

Much like with open rates, is your reader receiving the email at a time when they can do what you want them to do? Even if it is a good time to read the email, it might not be a good time to take the action. For example, if they are commuting on public transit, they might read an email inviting them to participate in your cool campaign, but they might not want to pull out their credit card on the bus. Or if you're sending an email to a prospective student during their lunch period, they might look at it, but they won't be able to sign up for the campus visit before talking to their parents. Think carefully about where they need to be in order to take the action you want them to take and adjust your send days and times accordingly.

MEASURING MORE THAN METRICS

Reporting on metrics is good to optimize the performance of your emails. But that's about all they measure: how well you've done your planning and writing.

Ultimately, what really matters is if email is helping you reach your actual business goals.

TIE YOUR EMAIL RESULTS TO STRATEGIC PRIORITIES

What are your organization's top priorities? How is that translated into goals? What are your strategies and tactics to hit those goals? What key performance indicators are being used to measure those goals? How does email contribute to those key performance indicators?

To prove the importance of your email operation, connect your email metrics to important key performance indicators for your organization. Here are some examples:

OUR EMAIL CALL-TO-ACTION (CTA)	KEY PERFORMANCE INDICATORS (KPIS)
Request more information	# of inquiries
Download a digital pack	Count of downloads
Start an application	# of started applications
Register for an event	# of attendees per year
Make a donation	Dollars raised

ASSESSING EMAIL PERFORMANCE AGAINST KPIS

How directly you'll be able to attribute an improvement in key performance indicators (KPIs) to email will depend on how sophisticated your email operation is. If you have extensive data collection and very savvy digital experts, you can get very close. If it's just you in a team of two, a spreadsheet will do.

Next we'll go through a few ways you can measure your emails' impact on KPIs, from the simplest (less accurate) to the most complex (most accurate).

CORRELATIONS

At the end of a cycle, take a look at your KPIs. Were they better than the year before? Sure, you can get away with saying that email contributed. But this method is problematic because email is likely not the only channel you used that year. However, you might be able to isolate some key moments and infer a greater correlation with email—especially if you can compare to previous years before your emails got better. Here are some of those moments to look for:

- Did you see more sign-ups to events where invites were only sent by email?

- Did you see fewer confused incoming calls as a result of information you sent proactively?

- If all other tactics were held equal, did you notice an improvement in dollars raised as a result of a changed email strategy?

You can level up this correlation reporting if there was a group of people who didn't get your emails, and if they acted differently than those who did.

A Lucky Accident

Dayana: Once upon a time, I was still working in an admissions office, and I noticed that deposits (students accepting) to our very popular nursing program were way below where they were the previous year at the same time. This was extremely concerning, because it is a program that needs a minimum number of enrolled students to run.

When digging into the data to understand what was wrong, I noticed that—due to a mistake in our email list queries—students with an offer of admission to nursing had not been receiving our yield emails (the emails that convince them to accept our offer of admission). While this mistake did not make my supervisor happy at all, it made *me* very happy, because I could show the impact our yield emails had on how many students accepted an offer of admission. We immediately started sending the yield email sequence, and the accepts jumped right up and even surpassed our enrollment goal.

CONVERSION TRACKING

Conversion tracking allows you to report a bit more confidently than correlating.

A conversion occurs when your reader takes a desired action from your email, like signing up for a webinar, downloading something, or making another transaction. Some of the ways to track conversions are link tracking, dedicated landing pages, and through integrated analytics software.

Direct Link Tracking

Instead of simply linking to your website in your email, use trackable links. These will record when a reader clicks on your link and the actions they take. You will need to use UTM parameters or tracking tokens appended to the URL. Google's Campaign Builder tool can help you create these tracking links easily (and for free!) and measure web traffic from a specific email campaign through Google Analytics.

Depending on how your operation is set up, you can also append specific codes to the end of your URLs to track all sorts of actions on your site. For example, nonprofit donation software can sync to emails with donation links that use specific "appeal" codes. With this tracking, organizations can tell how much money was raised from a single email campaign.

Dedicated Landing Pages

Creating landing pages specifically for email campaigns (as in, can't be accessed any other way) allows for precise tracking of visitor behavior and conversions. By directing email traffic to these dedicated pages, you can easily monitor how many visitors take the intended action.

Integrate Your Email Software with Analytics Tools

Your email software will probably have some tracking mechanism, but if you integrate email data with your web analytics, you can follow your reader's journey from email click to conversion on the website. Cool, right?! Now go make the web team your new best friends.

Ethical Tracking

Remember the Trust Triangle? It's essential that your conversion tracking methods comply with legal standards wherever you are. It's also essential that you tell your subscribers about the data you are collecting and how you are planning to use it.

Key Takeaways

- Single email metrics measure writing and formatting, while cumulative email metrics over time measure engagement with your readers and their trust in you as a sender.

- The true measure of your email success is against your past performance. Establish initial benchmarks for yourself (overall, by segment, by action) and continuously improve against your own past performance.

- Find a way to connect your email metrics to your organization's goals. Translate opens and clicks to actions and connect those actions to strategic priorities. Through this effort, demonstrate the importance of your email operation for your organization.

Chapter 9

AUDIENCE-CENTRIC OPERATIONS

Email marketing is one of the most effective channels for businesses to connect with people and drive conversions. But, to truly succeed in this space, the whole operation needs to adopt an audience-centric approach. In this chapter, we will explore the key considerations when setting up an email marketing operation to create personal, relevant, and timely email messages for your readers. By reaching the right person at the right time, you'll maximize engagement and achieve your goals.

Email operations involve how tools, messages, workflows, and staff member roles and responsibilities are organized. You will need to understand audience management and staff resourcing so your operation can build and send emails at scale.

Running an email operation requires technical and project management skills. You will need to monitor audience behaviors and leverage a variety of software. Your team must be skilled in writing, design, and attention to detail.

STAFF AND SKILLS

Running an email marketing operation requires a combination of technical expertise, creative skills, and strategic thinking. But anyone can write a good email. That ability relies mostly on human instinct and reading through this book.

For this section, we're focused on the various roles and skills necessary to build a competent email marketing team. Whether you are considering hiring new talent or developing existing staff, understanding the key roles and skills involved will enable you to create a capable team to execute successful email marketing campaigns.

KEY ROLES

A successful email operation has a diverse set of roles and skills to leverage. Roles will often overlap, and in small shops, you're wearing all the hats. Hiring or developing talent in email marketing management, campaign strategy, design, copywriting, data analysis, and technical proficiency will enable you to execute effective email marketing campaigns.

No matter your role, effective communication and collaboration within the team and across departments are critical if you dream of seamless execution and continuous improvement. By investing in the right staff and skills, you can create a competent email marketing team that drives engagement, conversions, and the overall success of your email marketing initiatives.

There are shared skills across roles:

- Strong interpersonal and communication skills to collaborate effectively with cross-functional teams

- Ability to manage multiple projects, meet deadlines, and adapt to changing priorities

Email Marketing Manager:

- Oversees the email marketing strategy and operations
- Develops campaign objectives, monitors performance, and implements improvements
- Manages the email marketing team and collaborates with other departments

Skills

- Familiarity with email service providers (ESPs) and marketing automation platforms
- Understanding of deliverability best practices, email authentication, and spam triggers

Email Campaign Strategist:

- Develops email marketing strategies aligned with business goals and target audiences
- Conducts market research, competitor analysis, and audience segmentation
- Creates comprehensive campaign plans, including content, timing, and segmentation strategies

Skills

- Proficiency in developing effective email marketing strategies aligned with business objectives
- Strong knowledge of email marketing best practices, industry trends, and compliance regulations

Email Designer:

- Designs visually appealing and mobile-responsive email templates
- Creates compelling graphics, imagery, and branding elements
- Collaborates with the content team to ensure consistent messaging and visual aesthetics

Skills

- Proficiency in graphic design tools to create visually appealing email graphics
- Knowledge of HTML and CSS to code and customize email templates

Copywriter:

- Crafts engaging and persuasive email copy
- Writes subject lines, preheaders, body content, and calls-to-action
- Adheres to brand voice and maintains consistent messaging across campaigns

Skills

- Excellent writing skills with the ability to create persuasive and engaging email copy
- Understanding of storytelling techniques, brand voice, and content optimization

Data Analyst:

- Analyzes email marketing metrics and provides actionable insights
- Tracks performance, identifies trends, and suggests optimizations
- Collaborates with other teams to leverage data for segmentation and personalization

Skills

- Strong analytical skills to interpret email marketing metrics and identify areas for improvement
- Proficiency in data analysis tools and techniques to track performance and measure campaign success

WORKFLOWS THAT WORK

Most teams struggle to find a sustainable workflow. We just reviewed all the roles and responsibilities that need to be carried out. It's time to quantify your work. How long does it take you to complete email tasks? How long will it take an email to get through your workflow from day one to send date?

We've found, on average, marketing teams put four hours into each email and can produce high volumes of email communication with a seven-day lead time. We're going to set strategy aside. Presume someone has done the good work to decide you need to send an email. They have been thoughtful about the audience and the content.

An optimized workflow to produce this email might look like this:

Step 1: Select a send date.

Step 2: Confirm audience details.

Step 3: Receive content.

Step 4: Build email.

Step 5: Test and preview.

Step 6: Receive OK to send.

Step 7: Schedule email.

We recommend removing content production from the email production workflow. Emails are often part of multichannel campaigns. Content creators can benefit from their own channel-agnostic production workflows.

Content placed into emails should be close to final. Design elements should be approved, and messages should be copyedited prior to the email build.

TOOLS AND SOFTWARE

We hope you took away this nugget from chapter 7—every organization can benefit from a shared email calendar. It's important to coordinate your email communication. Start with everyone in your organization who reaches out to the same audience you do. You want your messages to make sense to your reader. So, use a shared calendar to plan communication send dates.

Consider making rules for large communications. Pick specific dates and times to send to your entire audience and be consistent. Block these times on the calendar. Take space for the big communication pushes and make space for more targeted messages and calls-to-action.

For example, Cornell University's advancement marketing team sends a newsletter to all alumni each Tuesday morning. They also send a single call-to-action email each Thursday to large segments of their subscriber base. These dates are blocked on their shared calendar, signaling to partners that the five other days of the week are better times to send.

No-code database tools like Airtable offer calendar views, forms, and simple automations. With tools like these, your shared calendar can be used as an intake form for your email operation. Contributors can add their emails to the calendar through a short form. Set up an automated trigger for this action and your email team members can be alerted with next steps.

Email software can be simple or sophisticated. Ashley uses Mailchimp for her industry newsletter, and her higher ed team loves the bells and whistles that come with Salesforce Marketing Cloud. We know, at work choosing email software is often an organization-wide decision. Our tip? Whatever it is, make sure you find a good support community out there to help you with the technology when you get stuck.

Key Takeaways

- Email operations involve organizing tools, messages, workflows, and staff roles effectively. Staff resourcing and automating workflows are crucial components of building and sending emails at scale.

- A combination of technical expertise, creative skills, and strategic thinking is essential for running an email marketing operation. Strong interpersonal skills help with collaboration on the team and across departments.

- Streamline workflows, including steps like selecting a send date, confirming audience details, building the email, testing, and scheduling. Separate content production from the email production workflow for optimized efficiency.

CONCLUSION

From: Ashley & Dayana
Subject: Your turn: Send better emails 🖤

Our dearest reader,

All that's left now is for you to **go create better emails.**

Remember:

Email is about trust.
- Be authentic, empathetic, and logical.
- Consider your reader before you start writing.
- Create value above all.

You have 2 seconds.
- Get your point across with simple language and descriptive links.
- Put the most important words where the eyes will read.

Don't worry about perfect.
- Benchmark against yourself.
- Try, learn, and iterate.

It's time. You're ready. Go make good things happen with your emails.

Thank you for reading our book,
Ashley & Dayana

ACKNOWLEDGMENTS

Thanks to our friends at Cornell University for bringing us together and investing in us. And to the Cornell advancement marketing team for producing great work that inspires us.

To Erika Hall for encouraging us to write the thing. And to Joe Rinaldi for being our first fan. Thank you for taking our calls from Montreal.

To Mallory and Grant Willsea, and Joel Goodman, for being our design focus group and making us look good.

To the pros at Greenleaf Book Group: Steve Elizalde, Erin Brown, Liz Brown, Benito Salazar, Neil Gonzalez, Kyle Pearson, and Alyse Mervosh.

Thank you to the Council for Advancement and Support of Education (CASE) for inviting us to serve as Summer Institute faculty and create our curriculum.

To every person who has attended a workshop and given us feedback. You got us here.

Most of all, thank you to our husbands, Sandy Budd and Bruno Salcedo, for everything you do for us, Cora, and Romeo. 🐢

RESOURCES

Visit our website **emailbook.co** for additional resources. You'll find templates, workshops, podcast episodes, speaking information, and more.

FURTHER READING

ARTICLES

"Begin with Trust" by Frances X. Frei and Anne Morriss (2020) *Harvard Business Review*

"World Leaders in Research-Based User Experience" by Nielsen Norman Group, https://www.nngroup.com/articles/

ASHLEY'S NEWSLETTER

Get emails from Ashley Budd. 💌
https://ashleybudd.com/

BOOKS

Content Design by Sarah Winters (2017) Content Design London

Content Strategy for the Web by Kristina Halvorson (2009) New Riders

Design for Cognitive Bias by David Dylan Thomas (2020) A Book Apart

Everybody Writes: Your Go-To Guide to Creating Ridiculously Good Content by Ann Handley (2014) Wiley

How to Market a University: Building Value in a Competitive Environment by Teresa Flannery (2021) Johns Hopkins University Press

Influence: The Psychology of Persuasion by Robert B. Cialdini (2006 revised ed.) Harper Business

Just Enough Research by Erika Hall (2014) A Book Apart

Nicely Said: Writing for the Web with Style and Purpose by Nicole Fenton and Kate Keifer Lee (2014) New Riders

The Connected Campus: Creating a Content Strategy to Drive Engagement with Your University by Tracy Playle (2020) ContentEd

INDEX

ABOUT THE AUTHORS

ASHLEY BUDD and **DAYANA KIBILDS** are serious marketers with a soft spot for email. They first met as colleagues at Cornell University and spent the last decade working with higher education and nonprofit organizations. They share a love for teaching marketing in a practical and inspiring way.

Ashley Budd is senior director of advancement marketing at Cornell University. She lives in upstate New York with her family and two beloved peach trees. Ashley speaks regularly at marketing conferences and on podcasts. She consults with colleges, universities, and other nonprofit organizations. Together with Day, they coach and mentor new professionals. You can find them speaking about email and hosting workshops with teams across all kinds of industries.

Dayana (Day) Kibilds is a strategist at Ologie, a marketing and branding agency built for education. She's been working with higher education institutions worldwide for over a decade, pushing them to use their communications as tools for equity and access. She's an international keynote speaker on enrollment marketing, email strategy, productivity, and stakeholder management, and she's the host of Enrollify's *Talking Tactics* podcast. Day lives in Canada with her son, Romeo, and her husband, Bruno.